FOR
EVERYTHING
THERE IS
A SEASON

FOR EVERYTHING THERE IS A SEASON

Views From Middle Age Plus

by Carolyn Gray Thornton

Edited by Ellen Gray Massey

Skyward Publishing, Inc.
Dallas, Texas
www.skywardpublishing.com

Copyright 2002 by Skyward Publishing, Inc.

Publisher: Skyward Publishing, Inc.
              Phone (573) 717-1040
              Fax: 4130702-5141
              E-Mail: skyward@semo.net
              Web Site: www.skywardpublishing.com

**ATTENTION SCHOOLS
AND CORPORATIONS**

Skyward Publishing books are available at quantity discounts with bulk purchase for educational, business, or sales promotional use.

For information, write to:

Skyward Publishing, Inc.
Marketing
813 Michael Street
Kennett, Missouri 63857
(573) 717-1040
E-mail: skyward@sheltonbbs.com

*Dedicated to Michael, Shirley,
Mark,and Susan have
enriched their parents' lives.*

CONTENTS

1. A Time to Be Born

2. A Time to Laugh

3. A Time to Keep

4. A Time to Speak

5. A Time to Love

6. A Time for War

7. A Time for Peace

8. A Time to Dance

9. A Time to Heal

10. A Time to Die

ACKNOWLEDGMENTS

I would like to give thanks to two special people who helped make this book possible:

First, my husband, Lester Thornton, who encouraged me in my writing, insisted that I expand my readership by putting it in book form, and never complained when the meals were late, the house got dusty, or he had to batch for several days while I was off book-signing.

Next, my sister, Ellen Gray Massey, who left her own writing to help me with the hard work of editing and preparing the manuscripts for each of my books. I doubt that I would have ever had the courage to try such an endeavor without her technical support and sisterly encouragement.

Thanks go to Jeffrey Jackson, editor, and the staff at *The Nevada Daily Mail* for their patience and support.

And to my siblings, children, grandchildren, and great-grandchildren for tolerating me using them for material and still being proud enough of my work to share my book with their friends.

The wonderful people in Vernon County, Missouri, who started reading my columns eight years ago and who comments gave me the assurance that other people would also enjoy my writing.

And, to Shirleen Sando and Jim Harris of Skyward Publishing, Inc. who took a chance on an unpublished author by publishing and marketing my books.

INTRODUCTION

The only thing that is more fun than observing people and the way they react to life is to make observations about my own life and reactions. Writing about these things brings even more joy, especially when other people read my words and share their reactions with me.

I have had the privilege of writing a weekly newspaper column called "Middle Age Plus" for the past seven years. My column tells about the pluses of being past middle age and deals with the humor, loses and, changes that we encounter each day. In 1999, 101 of these columns were put together in a book entitled *A Funny Thing Happened on the Road to Senility* published by Skyward Publishing, Inc. These columns had been published in *The Vernon County Record* in Nevada, Missouri, a county seat town a hundred miles south of Kansas City.

When that newspaper sold out to *The Nevada Daily Mail*, also in Nevada, I continued writing the columns and have been requested by my readers to publish a second book. Wanting a slightly different format, but keeping the same up-beat look at my stage in life and the opportunities, problems, and joys that my age brings, I chose a division reminiscent of *The Book of Ecclesiastes*.

In the meantime, I have enjoyed sharing aspects of my life with my friends and large extended family both locally and across the nation through weekly columns and my first book, *A Funny Thing Happened on the Road to Senility: I Discovered the Joy of Middle Age Plus*.

I also write special feature articles for the Senior Page about people, places, things, and institutions that are over fifty years old. This has given me a wonderful opportunity to know many other people in this age group and to get an even deeper appreciation of the pluses not only of the age, but the pluses that those in this age group bring to our society.

As we share together an occasional laugh, tear, or smile at a memory, we appreciate that we are able to enjoy this precious stage of life. This book is a celebration of all of the times of our middle age plus lives.

PROLOGUE

Since I have reached the middle age plus years, I have discovered how much fun it is to share thoughts about my life through writing. As many of my readers are also in this same stage of life, together we can share our memories, our new experiences, and even enjoy hearing each other's 'organ recitals.' One of my long time friends and a faithful reader stated that you could tell when you are officially middle age plus when you find yourself eagerly describing to your friends your latest operation or infirmity. The key is seeing our body changes with humor and wonderment because inside we are still the young adult ready to conquer the world.

Our bodies are not the only things that change as we get older. Our neighborhoods, our friendship circles, and our priorities also see many changes. We look back at each time of our life and when we view it through our eyes, (which probably have received lens implants by now) we see the beauty and excitement in every time, even the final one.

I have been able to enjoy a new career in these later years. I have found people willing to read my scribbled thoughts after I brought my writing ambitions out of moth balls. With the urging of my husband, Lester Thornton, and my sister, Ellen Gray Massey, I have had the fun of writing two books about my age. I also co-wrote with my sister another book *Family Fun and Games: A Hundred Year Tradition*, Skyward Publishing Inc., about games our family has played since our parents hosted parties at the turn of the last century.

The memories brought forth from writing these books have made me realize that in spite of the Depression, World War II, Korea, Vietnam, and other catastrophes, these have really been very good years to experience. We are blessed with the current technology while still remembering clearly the days when we lived without electricity, running water, and paved roads. We have lost many of our long-time friends, but through this modern technology we are able to experience friendships across the globe through e-mail, chat rooms, television interviews, and airline travel. We have experienced the best of two ages. We don't need to dwell on the worst of those two ages because our perspective of age gives us the wisdom to know that 'this too shall pass.'

I am indebted to my parents for giving me the security to live without fear, to know that I am loved, and, by their example, to give me the instincts to chose wisely in my life mate and to enjoy my children. I had a happy childhood and have a good marriage. You can't ask for much more than that.

I end the book with a tribute to my mother that I wrote shortly after her death in 1969. All the other essays were published during the last decade as weekly columns in our local papers.

One of these days I will possibly really be old, but until then I plan to remain middle age plus and enjoy fully the great times of each season.

For everything there is a season and a
time for every matter under heaven:
a time to be born, and a time to die;
a time to plant, and a time to pluck up
    what is planted;
a time to kill, and a time to heal;
a time to break down, and a time to
    build up;
a time to weep, and a time to laugh;
a time to mourn, and a time to dance;
a time to cast away stones, and a time
    to gather stones together;
a time to embrace, and a time to refrain
    from embracing;
a time to seek, and a time to lose;
a time to keep, and a time to cast away;
a time to rend, and a time to sew;
a time to keep silence, and a time to
    speak;
a time to love, and a time to hate;
a time for war, and a time for peace.
                        Ecclesiastes 3:1-9

A TIME TO BE BORN

If birthing is a natural action
Then why the pain in each contraction?
The process merits no ovation
But the outcome calls for celebration.

I'M GLAD I WAS BORN!

"I love life and I want to live" are stirring words of a song by Paul Robeson. In my youth when I first heard the song, it filled me with excitement and joy. Belief in that philosophy didn't prepare me for attitudes I heard later in life.

"I didn't ask to be born" is a common argument given by teenagers who are resisting parental suggestions on behavior. In other words when they are being told what to do, how to act, or what they have already done wrong, they angrily protest that it is the parent's fault that there is this problem. If the parents hadn't begun the process of life-giving, there would be no child and, therefore, no need for this current discussion.

The same teen who so strongly protesting his existence in this discussion came into life eager to see what the world was like.

I remember being awed by our first son's desire to hold his head up and appear to be looking around while he was still in the glassed in nursery in the hospital. Michael can't tell me in his fiftieth year what he saw in that first look around, but he has never stopped being alert to what is going on around him, especially in the outdoors.

Through the years, I have marveled at the same impulse in our other children, grandchildren and great-grandchildren. I took grandson Jonathan's brother and sister, Chris and Alison, to see him in a Dallas hospital a few hours after his birth. While lying on his stomach, this strong little baby not only held up his head but held up his whole upper body with his arms while he looked out at the world. Since the great-grandchildren came in an era where newborns were laid on their back or side, the earliest glimpses of them didn't allow for the push-ups of the older children.

A toddler can't run fast enough to see, touch, grab, and taste everything that is in each room. The poor parent can't run fast enough to keep that little inquisitive body from experiencing all that life has to offer. The zest for life is so compelling that the little one literally wears out before satisfying each exploratory adventure.

Somewhere along the way the child decides it is not cool to show this joy in living. B-o-o-r-r-r-i-n-g becomes a much used word and attitude. Though carefully hidden in this new attitude, I firmly believe that the same zest and inquisitiveness remains.

Those of us who are middle age plus often renew this first born compulsion to see everything, only now we take time to enjoy and experience each aspect of life more slowly and fully. Minutes spent watching leaves skimming across the pond on an autumn afternoon are just as fulfilling as conducting an important business meeting. In spite of failing eyesight, arthritis and other ailments, we can still see and appreciate what life has to offer.

We may not be able to lay on our stomach, or if we can, it is doubtful we could hold up our head to look around, but life still looks pretty good to us from any position.

We didn't ask to be born, but, my we are glad that we were.

ROCKABYE BABY

Half a century ago when my husband, Lester, and I had our first children, the maternity ward was a sacred place, open only to certain family members at specific times. At announced hours, the father and other relatives saw the little one through the glass window of the nursery for a few minutes. The father waited for the birth in a waiting room and was told when the child was born, the gender, and size, but didn't get to actually touch or hold the baby until time to go home. The nurse brought the baby into the mother's room and laid the child on the bed. Finally, both parents were allowed to have physical contact while preparing the child for the trip home.

This was a memorable time, especially if home was some distance from the hospital, as ours was. Stops on the way to get formula and supplies prologed the time. In the front seat, the mother held the baby snugly in her arms while Dad drove, often trying to avoid potholes. Once home, the parents began the life-long care of this new individual after having had little contact during the hospital days. It was no wonder our first son had colic for three months, probably from the nervousness of his parents.

Last week my fifth great-grandchild was born here in Nevada. I have high praise for the staff in their treatment of family members. Our daughter and I were able to be with the soon-to-be mother right up to birth time. I stepped outside, but Shirley was able to be with Penny through the birth process. I was told to wait right outside the door so I could see the little one as soon as they took her to the nursery. Five minutes after the birth, I saw little Michaella. Though I expected then to wait in the waiting room a while, the nurses asked me to join them in the nursery as they took measurements and made footprints. Four generations of mothers and daughters shared the blessed event.

I didn't even see my own oldest children until they were several hours old, as I had been put completely under anesthesia. But here, along with Lester and other family members, I saw this little one in her first few minutes and held her before she was an hour old.

Our older children did not get to see their younger siblings or visit me until it was time to come home. At this newest birth, Marilyn sat on the bed with her mother and held her brand new sister. Earlier, a nurse had even unwrapped the infant to show the older child the tiny feet and hands and answered any questions she had.

The baby stayed in the room with her mother as long they both were contented. When the mother wanted to rest, the baby was cared for in the nursery.

The trip home was quite different from my time, also. The hospital will not release the child unless there is a car seat to protect her in the back seat of the car. A supplied diaper bag contained all the supplies needed for the first few days. Because this birth was by C-section, our granddaughter was able to stay in the hospital for three days. Her roommates, who had natural deliveries, were sent home when their children were twenty-four hours old.

In 1925 when I was born in the old Ammerman Hospital on the corner of Ash and Cherry, my mother stayed in bed at the hospital under the care of Miss Emma for ten days. Then she went home to a household of ten. Twenty- five years later, when our first ones were born, I was in the hospital for almost a week. This time was reduced to three days for our youngest child, but only with assurance that I would have help at home.

I'm glad I had some time to adjust to our expanded family before going home, but I'm sure the ten days bed rest of my mother was excessive and probably unhealthy. However, she and I did fine and stayed healthy, as will our newest little girl whom we all welcomed.

I am grateful that I shared this birth from outside the door and not from the delivery room table!

THE PUBERTY OF SENILITY

The Nevada Middle School has an excellent program called Girls' Empowerment. These monthly gatherings after school bring girls together with women in the community for discussions and social times together. Expert leaders discuss topics with the girls that might be troubling them and give guidance for handling problems.

At a recent meeting, I was privileged to be one of the adult women mentors to interact with the girls and listen to the presentations. Dr. Teri Loney talked with the girls about some of the psychological aspects of entering puberty. She asked if they sometimes felt that unexpectedly the body snatchers had taken their body and suddenly given them a new one.

Later when I was having refreshments with my group, one of the girls asked me the title of my book. When I said, "A Funny Thing Happened on the Road to Senility," she looked puzzled. She didn't know the meaning of the word, senility. In trying to explain the term to her, it hit us both that in many ways senility, or at least old age, was a good deal like puberty.

One day we take a good look at our bodies and realize that this isn't who we once were. We don't see signs of approaching maturity as the girls do; we struggle with the signs of approaching advanced age. The changes that happen are not just cosmetic, as they are not only outward signs with our young sisters. The changes hit every part of our being, physical, mental, psychological, and spiritual.

The young girls wonder what their lives will be like, what the final product of these body changes will bring. They become upset and confused because the same things don't affect them as they had in the past. Ditto to us middle age plus women. We wonder what the rest of our lives will have in store for us. We worry how the many bodily changes will affect our way of life. We find that we are upset by things that hadn't bothered us before and we are not upset by some things that formerly drove us up the wall.

The girls are dealing with new sanitation problems because of changes. Our older group also has comparable problems, now often portrayed on television commercials. We are always concerned about where the nearest restroom is and some are not secure enough in that situation to go to new or different places. It is safer to go where all the facilities are well known and have proper aids, such as grab bars.

Dealing with the opposite sex also brings changes in these two periods of life. The girls are troubled by changes in the way their former playmates are now reacting to them. Of course, their playmates are also going through puberty and facing body and psychological changes. Neither side knows just how to interact with the other in this new stage. So too does our generation have new rules to learn as we continue to live together with our 'playmate' of forty or fifty years. Our spouse or others in our peer group feel the affects of age as well. At different times couples often give up pastimes that both used to enjoy. The wife still enjoys travel but hubby wants nothing more than staying home. Or, the husband really enjoys putting out a big garden as always but the wife has no interest in preserving all that food. Sometimes roles have to be suddenly reversed when one partner must take over duties formerly performed by the other. But the biggest change is being home together all day. It has been said we married for better or worse but not for lunch.

We who are older remember well the struggles during the age of puberty. Those going through puberty don't have any concept of the feelings that approaching old age brings to both men and women. We each know that these are natural stages of life that lead to still other changes as time progresses. We don't always understand what is going on, or sometimes we understand too well. We older ones have a little advantage there in that we have seen more of life with more years to grasp the impact of the life span.

One thing is certain. The middle school girls don't want to be old. And we middle age plus folk wouldn't want to be their age again ever.

A FOWL MONTH AT BRONZE POND

My older sisters used to sing a popular nonsense song that went like this, "Let's all sing like the birdies sing, tweet, tweet, tweet, tweet, tweet. Let's all warble like nightingales, sweet, sweet, sweet." I have been singing this to myself this month as we are having the usual and unusual fowl happenings here by our pond.

First, our two pairs of Canada geese successfully hatched their broods although they never did learn to get along with each other. Anytime the older gander saw that the younger one was not patrolling his lady's nest, he tried to chase the goose off her nest. She squawked for help. The young gander returned and a fight ensued. Lester got tired of this. He began 'persuading' the old gander to stay on his side of the pond. It got so that we could just call out from the door, and he would return to his side.

The old pair successfully hatched six and the young pair only three, but by the next morning we could only see two. Within a day, all the old and young ones left our area for another haven somewhere. This departure has happened each year, and we have never been able to see where they go.

That should end the goose stories for the season, but three days ago another pair showed up once or twice a day with many loud squawks. The goose flies up into the new nest and stands or sits there for up to a half hour. The gander flies into the nest with her, flies away seeming to try to coax her to leave also, or he just swims around in circles at the base of the nest. We wonder if they are starting a late nest or playing house. Perhaps this is one of the original pairs who lost their little ones and are going to try again.

It's hard to get any work done for watching what the geese are doing next.

In the meantime, a deranged female cardinal has spent the last three week trying to knock herself silly on the east windows of our glassed-in porch. She has a regular pattern. She hits the tops windows with her beak, flies down to the lower level and finally hits the bottom panes. She will return to the feeder for a few minutes and repeat the same process. As soon as it is light in the morning, we hear the knocks on the window and know that she has survived another night ready to fight this 'foe' she sees reflected in our windows. Even on cloudy days, she keeps up her battle. She must think there are dozens of birds in our house because wherever she appears, there is one ready to fight back at her!

Less punitive are several hummingbirds that contest the spouts at our feeder. Occasionally an oriole will also come for a sip. I had an oriole feeder one year without attracting a single bird. This year one is coming when I don't have things ready.

Turtle doves or mourning doves have been singing to us for several weeks now as a sure sign of warm weather. Lately, we hear an owl at night.

To cap off all these feathered friends, a mocking bird flies to the highest spots in the yard to sing his melodies. The top of the electric pole, the television antenna, and the tallest trees are usually populated with this little persistent singer. I wonder how he ever gets anything to eat or what his mate is doing while he is singing his heart out.

Just in case one of these birds is not performing for us, we have a bird clock that produces a different bird song at each hour.

Back to my sisters' songs. If I'm not "Listening to the Mockingbird," or watching the "Red Red Robin," then I am singing like the birdies sing, "Tweet, tweet, tweet, tweet, tweet." But I draw the line at fighting my own image in the glass. Being middle age plus has taught me to stay away from images in mirrors or glasses.

Excuse me while I go fill the bird feeder again!

DOUBLE DIP PEOPLE?

There is a lot of talk about cloning a person to have an exact duplicate. I don't want to get into the whole subject of whether it is right or wrong to do that. I just know that I wouldn't want to have a duplicate of myself running around. If I could improve upon me, that might be different, but it would be creepy to see a younger version of me going through the same things I did.

This model couldn't be identical because the environment would be different. Even with the same house and the same community, it would not be the same. Unless you cloned the entire family and community members and had a time machine put the clock back, the results in my clone would not be the same as in me. When we think how often a chance meeting has changed us, we know that no two lives can be the same. When an outsider steps inside our family circle, nothing is ever the same again. Each of us has some influence on each person we meet, and each person we meet changes us somewhat. So I don't think cloning will ever produce another Carolyn who will end up just as I am.

When I think back to the modern devices of each of the decades I have lived through, I can see that many of our advances were not as terrific as we thought at the time. That even goes for some medical and scientific advice that was not always correct.

Our first baby died at eight days due to a birth defect. After having a perfectly healthy son, our next daughter had a slight disability which my pediatrician said could be linked to the problems of our first daughter. He couldn't say for sure, but he advised against us having more children since we already had a nice family. We took his advice, but then had two more children while using two different types of birth control, obviously unsuccessfully.

These two children are as bright, good looking, and healthy as any person could be. I can't imagine what life would be like without them in our family. Though their coming caused us a little concern during the pregnancies, I developed a fatalistic attitude. If I wasn't supposed to have these children, the birth control wouldn't have failed. That was not really my theology, but it kept me from worrying too much during those nine months.

The doctor's advice was well meaning, the birth control methods were approved, but we didn't benefit from either of them. We benefitted because they were each inadequate.

Our family of four, Michael, Shirley, Mark, and Susan, spread out over eleven years, is just right for us, and we have never regretted for an instance that the plans were not fool proof. In fact, Susan once said that our family was just right because the older three learned about taking care of babies and little children from helping with her raising, and she learned the same things from helping with her nieces and nephews.

So, if I was cloned, would I have the same children? Not unless I also had a cloned husband or that Lester had lived long enough to be the mate of my clone. I don't think I would like that. I know I wouldn't. Even if it were a clone of me, I wouldn't want to share my husband. So, if my clone didn't have the same children that the original me had, she wouldn't be a duplicate of me at all.

Each of the children have changed me, taught me, inspired me, and worn me out at different times. Those actions have shaped what I am. For better or worse, I am a daughter, sister, niece, grandchild, aunt, wife, mother, grandmother, great-grandmother, and friend of specific people who are part of me. My thoughts, language, interests, even my abilities are what they are, in part, because of these people who are more numerous than I can count.

So while thinking about the whole idea of cloning and birth control, I wonder about my own mother. Since I was the youngest of eight children, born when my mother was forty-three, I seriously doubt that I was a planned baby. I'm sure I was born the usual way and wasn't a clone of some earlier Carolyn. After seven kids, who would even consider cloning an eighth?

THE LONGEST WORD IN THE ENGLISH LANGUAGE

An exciting thing happened to me today. My youngest great-granddaughter smiled at me. That doesn't seem like such a big deal when I have three other great-granddaughters who all smile at me often. But this was the first time this little one had smiled at me in her seven weeks of life. That smile, like the first smiles of each little baby, signify the beginning of a personality that will respond to others.

Have you ever seen an adult who will not light up immediately when a very small baby smiles at them? Not only do we smile back at the child, but we make some happy exclamation such as, "Did you see that? She smiled at me."

I have maintained that smiling is a special gift given to the human race. No other animal smiles, although some dogs almost appear to be smiling when they are panting with their tongue hanging out. We know that the dog's smile is in the wag of its tail as the cat's is in its purr. But the facial expression we call a smile is reserved for human beings. Therefore, when Michaella smiled at me, I rejoiced at her entrance into the pleasures of human interaction.

When I was a youngster in 4-H Club, we had a song we often sang at meetings. The words went like this, "It isn't any trouble just to s-m-i-l-e. It isn't any trouble just to s-m-i-l-e. And if you have a trouble, it will vanish like a bubble, if you only take the trouble just to s-m-i-l-e." The song continued with "g-r-i-n grin," then "l-a-u-g-h," and finally "ha-ha-ha-ha-ha." By then the group was convulsed in laughter.

I have remembered that song for years and often try it on myself when things look a bit dark for some reason. It always works, and I end up smiling myself. I find I smile now when I see some unexpected spot of beauty, the first bloom on a nurtured plant, a hummingbird coming to the feeder early in the morning, or my first sighting of the new moon each month. I always have a smile for the little ones in our family, feeling rewarded when they return one to me.

Another childhood memory proclaims the word smiles to be the longest word in the English language. It has a 'mile' between the first and last letters! My adult mind wants to add that it may be the strongest word in the English language because it can overcome anger. Sometimes after an argument our faces feel almost frozen with clenched jaws and tightened lips. If something can bring forth a smile, then suddenly all those muscles relax and the world seems much brighter.

Some of my song books of golden oldies echo these thoughts. Titles such as "Let a Smile Be Your Umbrella on a Rainy, Rainy Day," or "Smile When You're Feeling Blue," remain favorites for years because we all crave the pleasure that accompanies a smile.

The walls of my combination guest room and office are lined with pictures of loved ones in my family. The ones I like the best are portraits that show a smile. Some of the older photographs of grandparents, aunts, and our parents show rather stern expressions. This leaves an erroneous image in our minds of the personality of those ancestors. I never knew my paternal grandparents and every picture of them shows stern, forbidding looks on their faces. Therefore, I am surprised when my older siblings tell of fun things they did with these grandparents. I believe them, but the image in the large framed portrait of my grandfather is more firmly fixed in my head than the second hand stories of their personalities.

Now that picture-taking is a very common occurrence, we are not intimidated by a camera being focused on us. Perhaps that is why we can be more natural and show a little teeth as our oldest great-granddaughter does as she tries so hard to be cooperative that she overdoes the smile.

Most of us won't have the shock of being told to "Smile, you're on Candid Camera," but we are always being watched by someone. The day will go better if you share a smile or two with those around you.

THE BIRDS AND BEES ARE GETTING BUSY

Spring brings us many signs of new birth, a happening that is dear to the heart of all of us. But I have an admission to make. One of the best things about being middle age plus is you can enjoy and celebrate new birth all around you but don't have to worry about it happening to you! I have nothing against little babies. I have had my share including grandchildren and great-grandchildren, but I certainly don't want a little one of my own, full time.

It is fun to watch various kinds of parents with their little ones. Right now we are enjoying our nesting geese. We think it is at least the eighth year they have nested with us. Last year a second pair tried to run them out, but Lester put up a second nest and they both hatched their brood in spite of frequent squabbles and fights. This year no other pair has attempted to take up residence since very early in the mating season when 'our' gander ran off another pair that dared to land on our pond.

At first our pair commuted back and forth from our pond where the nests are to a new pond on the family farm next door. Later, the goose has stayed on the nest full time except for very brief breaks to eat a little and take a quick dip. In the meantime, the gander patrolled the pond and stayed close by. At this stage, nature doesn't provide an equality in the nesting/hatching process for our feathered friends, but once the goslings hatch, the gander gets very involved in their care.

We also have a pair of squirrels who have been helping themselves from our bird feeder. I recently heard that a way to avoid the problem of squirrels eating the birds' food was to rename the feeder. Simply call the contraption the bird *and* squirrel feeder and enjoy both species. Lately we see only the male squirrel. We wonder if his mate is raising some young somewhere nearby, although we haven't spotted her if she is. We have lots of trees around so there is no way we could be sure just where the possible nursery is. I only hope that when the little ones are out and about, the parents will bring them by for us to see. We might even need to put up an additional bird and squirrel feeder.

Our gold finches have returned with their plumage turned to yellow. I have never been sure if that color is to attract mates or if it is to blend in with blossoms and leaves. Whatever the reason, we love to watch their quick actions.

Of course the robins, cardinals, blue jays, and meadow larks join the throng each day and some of the winter birds are still here. I have set up a working table on our east enclosed porch so that I can work while watching all this wildlife. It's even better if I can open the windows to hear the birds' songs.

Our flowers are also coming to life. I don't know

if you can call them baby flowers, but the crocus have come and gone, the daffodils are beginning to show their colors and the lilac, redbud, and forsythia tell us that they have finished their winter sleep and will soon join us in full array.

As the process of new birth continues all around, we have found ways in our retirement to have new birth of our own. We are not expecting another child, or at the present not even another great-grandchild. We have given birth to new habits and new pastimes. We eat when it is convenient and not necessarily at eight, twelve, and six. We sleep late some days and get up early on others. We share some interests while each has separate hobbies. The best thing about these new creations is that we don't have to get up at night with them, save money for college, or worry about what is happening to the car.

In middle age plus we can casually say, "We've been there, done that, got the tee shirt." Of course the tee shirts say, "The World's Best Grandmother" and "The World's Best Grandfather."

NEW EYES, OLD GLASSES

Cataract surgery is becoming so common that many middle age plus people have a large group of friends to compare notes with when discussing their surgery. Not too many years ago people dreaded the operation because of the restrictions afterwards. The patient had to stay almost immobile for several days, not leaning over, turning in bed, or doing any work for a couple of weeks.

Now the process is much shortened. As an outpatient, the patient goes home within a few hours. After a return visit the next morning, almost all restrictions are removed.

You may have guessed that I recently had this surgery on each eye, one at a time. Since it occurred over the holiday period when there was also extreme cold and much snow, I used my 'condition' as an excuse to stay home from several events and modified our family gathering a bit. The worst part of the whole event was the recuperation period when I had new eyes but old glasses.

My vision was helped so much that wearing my old glasses was out of the question. I do not need correction except for close work. I thought that would be okay. I bought a cheap pair of magnifying half glasses to put on when I needed to read something. My problem was that I never had them with me when I needed to read. Leaving them perched on the end of my nose simplified the problem, but I was foolish enough to buy a pair with horn-rimmed frames thinking they would take more rough wear and tear. When I perched the glasses on the end of my nose, the whole world had a reddish brown stripe running across it. This was so disconcerting that I didn't wear any glasses at all when driving.

Not needing glasses to drive is wonderful since I no longer have problems at night, and I can read the highway signs at quite a distance. My problem comes when I need to see what is on the dashboard. Most of the words and letters are large enough or well-lighted enough that I have no problems. But the mileage marker is impossible to read unless I put on my 'cheaters.' When following someone's directions to their home, I need to see when I have gone the one mile or three miles to a certain corner.

In our part of the county, since the roads are marked off conveniently in mile squares, it is easy to know when I've gone a mile. Not all of the places I visit in search of my stories have this convenience. Around the rivers and in the hilly areas, I need to read my odometer. This is really a minor inconvenience for the privilege of having much better eyesight.

My biggest thrill came when I drove home from Raytown at night. Night driving in the city had been a nightmare for me for the past couple years. This trip was a breeze. The headlights of oncoming cars and the overhead and roadside lights were no problem. When I got on Highway 71, the straight shot home, I was very excited to see much of the surrounding countryside. A half moon helped but hadn't made all of the difference.

Another minor problem was the required periods of regular eye drops. I have always been a blinker. If I know a drop is coming at my eye, I have a very hard time keeping my eye open. Since it became inconvenient to always have a partner administer the drops, I gave myself the four-times-a-day treatment. I hope the material in eye drops is good for my complexion as I got as much on my cheeks as I did in my eyes.

I now have new glasses to go with my new eyes and I work crossword puzzles with the same spectacles that I wear to drive my car.

I'll be seeing you!

GIVING BIRTH IN YOUR SEVENTIES

In my writing, I have occasionally shared the sad news about the loss of a friend or a loved one. Instead, I would like to share the good news about a birth. You see, even in middle age plus, I have given birth. The labor was quite long for a birth, but it was a pleasurable labor and the only pain, as in many births, was at the very end when the exact arrival was uncertain.

I have given birth to a book. This book is a selection of what the publisher (Skyward Press from Dallas), my sister, Ellen Gray Massey, who is the editor of the book, and I decided were the best of the six years of weekly columns I have written under the title, *Middle Age Plus*. I will have to admit that some of my very favorite columns were not included because they would have had meaning only for those in Vernon County. We tried to make the book interesting to people of any age in any type of community. But those who are also in my age group and who have experienced living in a county like ours will probably get more enjoyment from the book.

The process of publishing a book is quite different from my expectations when I was nine years old and crawled up on the smokehouse roof with my Big Chief tablet to write a novel. That novel never got written nor did any other novels get finished. I began to see that my gift, combined with my laziness, was more for short essay-type thoughts on life. In different communities where we lived, I wrote for various newspapers and once even had a column over the radio in Butler, Missouri. However this series of *Middle Age Plus* columns has lasted the longest and has generated the most interest. Maybe because more of us are becoming middle age plus?

Back to the publishing process--I was very lucky that Ellen was attending a writer's workshop where she met Jim Harris who had purchased a small, special interest publishing company in Dallas, Texas. We had been working on a manuscript of my book which she had with her. Jim liked what he read. It isn't usually this easy, but was a case of my sister being in the right place at the right time. Skyward Publishing, Inc. is specializing in books that fit special niches. My book fit a niche so the process of getting it into print began.

The most agonizing part was trying to decide which columns to use. Some which I felt had little value were favorites of the others. Some of my special favorites were discarded. But all in all we agreed that our final selection was good.

I had assumed all along that the book would retain the title I had given it, that is *Middle Age Plus*. However the powers that be, wanted a more catchy title. A title of one of the essays was "A Funny Thing Happened on the Road to Senility." The president of the publishing company saw that title and e-mailed Jim Harris that she had found the perfect title. He agreed, so that settled that question, which I hadn't realized in advance was even a question.

It would seem that everything would be smooth sailing now that the book was named, the contents approved, and the contract signed. What I was not aware of was the long process of designing the cover, and arranging the captions and illustrations. When that was finished then my book had to wait its turn at the printers and even then was delayed further by a glitch in a computer disc so that a whole chapter had to be returned. Finally, books were shipped to me in time for my first-ever book signing at the office of the *Nevada Daily Mail*.

Like all proud parents, I will be happy to show off the results of this birth anytime. I might 'just happen' to have a few in the trunk of my car. Giving birth can be lots of fun if you can survive the long wait. At least I won't have to get up at night with this birth product.

Section Two

A TIME TO LAUGH

Come laugh with me so you can see
The one I'm laughing at is me.

TRAINING SENIOR HUMANS

As Dictated to Carolyn Gray Thornton
by Wynkum, Blynkum, and Nod

The other day when we were eating our supper off of a newspaper in our 'cat house,' we noticed an article written by one of our humans, Carolyn Gray Thornton. It was "When Your Pet Becomes a Senior Citizen." We were slightly interested in this although we are only eleven years old which makes us about the same age as our humans. However, we think that we are in better shape than they are.

Since our female human (we call her Carolyn) is pretty busy these days, we offered to write her column for her. We didn't volunteer to help her out, but we wanted to have a chance to explain our training methods which we have used rather successfully for all of our nine lives.

When there are dogs in the family, humans read articles to learn how to train them. If you are lucky enough that cats choose to live with you, the training is reversed. We are happy to share our techniques with the public in hope that some kitten will eat her supper off of the newspaper and learn from us.

There are four basic tricks we must teach our humans.

1. Heeling: Proper cats will want their favorite human to obediently follow behind them as they lead the way to the refrigerator or the food cabinet. The best way to insure that the humans heel correctly is to constantly walk right in front of them, criss-crossing back and forth in their way so that the easiest thing for them to do is just follow behind. Always do this with a fully erect tail and possibly some oral commands to draw attention to the trick they are mastering. The erect tail clearly shows the human who is in charge here and will set the tone for other obedience tricks such as placing the desired food where we can enjoy it.

2. Sit: A human must be taught to not move around constantly but to sit in a chair or lie on a bed often. We teach Carolyn this trick by instantly getting into her lap when she sits or lies down. Then we refuse to move. Since we are approaching middle age plus, and we know she is already there, we feel these long rest periods are good for all of us. Even if the chair is in front of the computer, it is our duty to sit in her lap to keep her resting.

3. Fetch: With patient training most humans can be taught to provide what is necessary for feline comfort. If the food is not what we really want at that moment, we sniff the dish and walk away in disgust. Most humans will quickly offer another type of nourishment that suits our taste better. If this doesn't happen immediately, using the silent meow treatment will usually work. Just open your mouth as if to protest with a meow, but because of your weakness due to lack of food, don't actually make a sound.

This training maneuver is very successful.

4. Open: The last and probably the most important trick to teach is Open. Even though cats are naturally superior in most ways, our lack of opposing thumbs makes it hard for us to open and close doors. (We don't really care whether they get closed or not, but we need to have our humans trained to open them at our command.) First, rise from the lap, couch, or bed, stretch, and walk leisurely to the door. If it is not opened immediately, return to the nearest human, rub against her legs. (This is especially effective in shedding season when the human is wearing pants!) Purr loudly and return to the door. A wistful look from the door back to the human will usually complete the training session making future occasions move much speedier.

As in all training practices, remember to give approval or some treat when the humans have correctly performed the feat. Purrs and affection will make them eager to please you the next time. But always be sure that they know just who is the boss!

PERSONAL LOST AND FOUND PILE

Since I have become middle age plus, I have found that I often misplace things. Maybe I should say I lose things, but it really isn't a matter of actually losing something. I just can't find it. My father used to say that in our house we had a place for everything and nothing was in its place. I'm not sure now that I even have a place for everything. I guess I do, but it is the same place—a place to pile stuff until I can find another place to put it away. Since I never get around to finding that other place, the pile gets deeper until I have to start over. The value of this process is that most things I need are somewhere in that mess. If I look long enough, I will find whatever it is that I need. The problem is that on the way to finding the searched-for item, I run across a bunch of other things that should have had my attention days or weeks ago.

Depression can set in very quickly under these circumstances, so it is better not to tackle the pile. It is surprising how often things get taken care of without my attention.

In spite of becoming accustomed to misplacing

things, this morning I was really shocked when I looked into the mirror and saw that I had lost something very important. I lost my lips. The last time I put lipstick on, they were there, very thin to be sure, but there. But this morning in the dim dawn light I looked and they were gone. Just disappeared into a straight line across the bottom of my face.

I could purse my mouth in such a way that I could see remnants of those facial features from the past, but in my relaxed mode they were gone. I don't know why I used the term, relaxed. I was anything but relaxed. After all, a very important part of my face wasn't there anymore. I don't think calling the sheriff or the FBI could have helped because the thief who took my lips was Father Time. He is immune from prosecution in spite of all the damage he has done over the years to those lucky to have lived long enough.

I tried to reconstruct the scene of the crime. Just when did the theft take place? I'll admit that I have been too busy lately to worry much about make-up, but I think I would have noticed something. I couldn't pinpoint any exact time when I last saw my lips.

I remember using them frequently to kiss my loved ones, to form words as I talked, and to usher food into my mouth. But I didn't really see them during these moments. I found myself chewing on my upper lip just now when I was trying to get my thoughts in order, but I don't have a mirror nearby to see if they have returned.

Sour people have been described as tight lipped, or thin lipped. I hope I don't fit that description but maybe my lips do. How can I avoid that look? Putting on more lipstick might help. It could disguise the problem. Or it could draw attention to it. With my luck, the lipstick would probably look like a thin red line under my nose.

I think I have found the solution, however. When I smile, I draw my mouth back in such a way that the absence of lips is not noticeable. The same thing happens when I talk. I guess I will have to go around smiling and talking up a storm so that no one will notice my loss.

Since I wear glasses, need a hearing aid, have wrinkles and brown spots on my face, perhaps no one will notice that I have one more defect. I will keep smiling and when you smile back at me, then neither of us will have to notice the presence or absence of lips.

Maybe I should go look in the most recent pile of stuff I have collected. Maybe along with all the advertisements, newsletters, and bills I will be lucky enough to find my latest lost item. But if I don't find them, and you meet me and notice the flaw, please don't give me any lip about it.

AN OUNCE OF PREPAREDNESS
IS WORTH A POUND
OF POTATOES

I was planning to have the family over for the traditional Easter meal right after church services. We were also planning to arrive at the church early for the Easter breakfast and service. Of course, I had to hide a few goodies from the Easter bunny so they would be ready when we came home. Since we also needed to be finished eating and cleaning up by two o'clock in order to attend a great-grandchild's fifth birthday party at her home north of Adrian, I made several advance preparations.

I boiled and deviled the eggs, made an angel food cake complete with jelly bean decoration, and got out all the dishes needed for the dinner. The directions for the ham said to put it in a shallow baking pan with one cup of water and seal it tightly with aluminum foil. I didn't want the ham itself to sit out all night, but I prepared the pan, added the water, tore off the desired amount of aluminum foil and placed it on the counter in a handy spot.

My menu also included baked potatoes. Knowing that they didn't need to be refrigerated, I scrubbed and prepared them for baking and put them in the oven. Then I had a bright idea. I could go ahead and set the timer on the oven so that in the morning all I had to do was put the ham in the pan and pop it in the oven.

All this advance preparation would be a good example for the expected family members. Their busy life styles sometimes made them put aside some traditional celebrations because there wasn't time. I felt that I would be able to show them that with planning ahead, we can do most things. I relaxed for a good night's sleep.

Early on Easter morning, three a.m. to be exact, I woke up with the overpowering odor of baked potatoes. In my sleepy state I couldn't figure out why this should be and decided I probably was dreaming since my last activities the night before had centered around the potatoes. I dozed off again for a while and then suddenly sat up in bed. The odor was very insistent and smells don't usually enter into our dreams.

I hurried into the kitchen where, sure enough, there was a very hot oven with several very well-baked potatoes inside. I turned off all the controls, bemoaning that my time control evidently no longer worked properly. I was concerned how I could have the ham baked and ready to eat if I couldn't count on the timer.

In the morning, I realized my error. The timer on the oven has a twelve-hour cycle, not the twenty-four hours of an actual day. I had set the timer to go on at 11:15 (thinking a.m.), and to go off at 12:15

(thinking p.m.). But I did this at 10 p.m. the night before I needed the heat. To complicate matters, in my hurry, I confused the start and stop times so the oven was obligingly baking away for a scheduled eleven-hour bake that I had mistakenly ordered.

The potatoes in question were *very* well baked. I fact, they were merely hollow brittle shells. Out of curiosity I broke one open to see only some brown ragged remnants of a good meal.

Fortunately, I had extra potatoes. I hurriedly cleaned them to join the ham in a properly set oven awaiting our return from church.

Though the family enjoyed the meal, I did not give my intended lecture on the advantages of advance preparation. I had too much fun telling the story to my friends at the church breakfast to feel bad about my wasted energy, potatoes, and electricity.

Almost every woman at the table had a similar story to tell of a wonderfully planned meal that didn't turn out quite as expected. One woman, known for being an excellent cook, was being taken out for Easter dinner because of a similar disaster at the last holiday when she forgot to turn on the controls after preparing and putting everything in the oven.

Maybe that is the very best type of advance preparation—having the family take you out to eat because they no longer trust your memory!

UNCLUTTER YOUR LIFE

I attended a meeting last week that was designed to help us 'unclutter' our lives. The suggestions in the program paid much attention to the organization of the workplace. I came away thinking that I had found the answers to my cluttered life. No longer would I spend hours looking for a piece of paper that I had just laid down. I will follow the rules and become more efficient as I write my articles, do my daily business, and attend to responsibilities of different offices that I hold.

One of the first rules was to get rid of the clutter on your desk. The first circle area (called Area A) should be free of anything except what you are actually working on at the moment. The next area (creatively called Area B) would contain only the tools needed to do the work. This would involve the telephone, computer, pens, and pencils. There was a third area (Area C) but for the life of me I can't remember what was supposed to be there. My problem was with the suggestion to get these areas cleared for the proper use of Areas A and B by putting everything on the floor.

My mind got so boggled thinking about where I

could find another spot on the floor, that I completely missed Area C. But it didn't matter. Inspired to do something about my clutter, I was ready to take action.

To start, I bought two things to get me organized. One is actually called an organizer. The other is an expanding portable file folder. I got the organizer at a very reasonable price, and when I got home I found out why it was so inexpensive. It was for last year. I could still use it by writing in the correct dates for this year, but since I haven't had time to make those corrections yet, I laid the pretty organizer front and center on my desk where I won't neglect to do something about it. I think it is lying in Area A.

The folding file carrier will be just what I need to take to meetings where I am expected to have many different facts ready during the session. There are little tabs to stick in perforations at the top of each section to identify what papers will be nestling in each particular section.

The folder also had a stuck-on commercial label on the front under a protective plastic shield that I needed to remove so I would look more professional when I pulled out my folder. The trouble was, the sticky label was really a good sticky label that didn't come off easily. In trying to remove it, I encountered several problems that involved getting a knife, a damp cloth, and two band-aids. I will not go into details. You get the picture.

Since it is hard to file papers with band-aids on your fingers, I postponed transferring the materials from my desk and nearby table top into the new folder. After all, I didn't want the papers to be smudged with blood. So I turned my attention to putting all the stuff from the table and desk tops on the floor.

I already have two piles of books in the knee hole of my desk for easy reference when the spell check and I don't agree, or to look up a fact that I should have remembered easily. Since I have to move the table the computer keyboard is on to file my articles in the file drawer, if I put anything on the floor there, it would get messed up, torn, or lost for good each time I move the table. I keep a big wastebasket next to my work area to put in all the opportunities to win a million dollars that I receive each day. But since we recycle all our papers, I have to organize the waste paper into that which is icky and must be thrown away for good, that which can be recycled, and that which is on slick paper and should go with the magazine recycling pile.

On the other side of my desk is the door to the room. Any more piles of papers there would be a fire hazard. Under the beds (my office doubles as a guest room) is a wonderful place to stash stuff, except that it is already full of games, pictures to put in my picture file when I get around to it, and more books. I guess I cannot put any of this desk top clutter on the floor, even temporarily. Actually it fits pretty well right where it is. I have gotten used to it being there.

But I really did make a lot of progress after the meeting. I bought the organizer and the folding file carrier. They will be very helpful when I get around to using them. When you are middle age plus, everything doesn't have to be done right away. The organizer is already a year off. If I fix it now, one whole month will be wasted. Maybe I'll wait until next year to start using it.

MY CHINNY CHIN CHIN

My late sister, Miriam, was always proud of her chin. She had a rather square chin which was almost rugged for a woman. She was proud of it because it didn't get the 'witchey look' (her term) as she got older. It retained its rugged square look all of her life.

The chins of more petite women who have dainty little faces with pointed chins tend to age in a different way. As their faces thin and perhaps the teeth wear down a bit, (horses aren't the only animals whose teeth grind down, you know) their chins become even more pointed, making the faces appear older. Miriam often remarked that she was glad she didn't have that particular sign of aging. She had her share of other signs, of course, but she pointed out this feature to me quite often. We would meet one of our older friends and after the woman had left, Miriam would ask me if I had noticed her chin. Usually I had not.

Recently I met a new friend whose chin was so pointed that I couldn't help but notice. Since this woman was probably in her sixties, I imagine that it had become more prominent in the last decade. Of course, I didn't ask her or mention the fact, but I did silently 'tell' Miriam, "Yes, I noticed her chin."

The woman had a wonderful smile, was lively, and good company, but because of this emphasis from my sister, I couldn't help but notice her chin.

Then I came home and was putting on lipstick using the bathroom mirror which had brighter lighting. As I turned my lips inward to spread the lipstick more evenly, I caught a glimpse of a rather prominent chin. Since Miriam had never remarked about this attribute on me (and she would have if she had noticed it), I had not given a second thought to that part of my face in spite of her many remarks about chins. But here I was peering into the mirror and turning my head each way to see. Do I really have the beginnings of that 'witchey look'? The tension of the moment made me clamp my teeth together even harder and press my lips together in deep thought.

Lester always says I can't do anything without holding my mouth just right. If I thread a needle, I not only hold the needle up to the light to see better, I purse my lips tightly together as if that tension will make the thread go the proper way. Each time I feed a child, my mouth opens with every bite that I get into the child's mouth. When trying to remember a name or a phone number, I tend to bite my lower lip.

Sometimes I tend to push my lips out to aid in some task. Other times I pull them in to the edge of my teeth. Whatever I am doing seems to involve my lips in some way. So that particular moment when I noticed the chin under my lips was no different. I had my lips sucked in together.

Sure enough, my chin was protruding more than

it had in the past. I came into the bedroom where I had my high school graduation picture and examined my chin at that age. Since it didn't look much different from our golden wedding picture, maybe I am just imagining the change.

That night I watched the *Tonight Show* with Jay Leno. His obvious trademark chin hasn't caused any drawbacks to his career. I decided to let the matter rest. After all, there are many more important things in life than what my chin looks like. Having good teeth inside that chin comes to mind as more important. Also being able to use that same chin to eat, smile, and laugh are far more important to me than how it looks.

I enjoy meeting new people and learning all about them. I like to offer my hand and introduce myself while kidding myself that I will remember their names. But I think in the future when I do meet a new friend I will be a little cautious. I don't want to lead with my chin!

DON'T WORRY BE HAPPY

When you get older, you are not supposed to care as much what other people think about you. Your age should have given you the self confidence to do your own thing and not worry if it meets approval of others. Right? Well, maybe I'm not old enough yet for this. Perhaps like the woman in *The Mikado*, I am not sufficiently decayed because I get cold chills when I find I mess up something or forget to do something I agreed to do.

The worst thing is (as I am getting sufficiently decayed) I find that I do mess up a bit more than in the past. And I know I forget more easily. I got a letter in the mail today telling me that I hadn't sent in a form that was due a month ago. I didn't forget to send it. I didn't know I was supposed to send it because I missed the training meeting. My first thought was, "What will they think of me?" I began composing a long letter telling all the reasons I am late with the form. Then decided I might make a better impression if I just said I'm sorry to be late and let it go at that. I wonder which way would make the letter writers approve of me?

This started me thinking about other times recently that I have been concerned about what someone else thought of me. When I stayed in a motel recently, I messed up the bath towel so the maid wouldn't think I hadn't taken a bath. I hadn't. I had taken one right before I drove to the motel, and I left early the next morning. I will probably never see the maid, but somehow it didn't seem right to have just a wash cloth and a hand towel used. Now, mind you, I wouldn't share this with just anyone because it makes me look paranoid. I knew you all wouldn't think badly of me for admitting such actions.

I became tickled recently at an inappropriate time and tried to cover my laugh with a coughing spell. Instead of making people think I was behaving badly, I let them think I was exposing them all to a virus or worse. So I tried to make that look better by mumbling to a neighbor that I must have gotten sort of choked.

I can't eat onions or garlic because they do unspeakable things to my insides. At covered-dish dinners or when I am a guest at someone's home, if I find there are onions or garlic in a dish, I try to make it look like I had eaten some of it by spreading it around on the plate a bit. Some friends who know my dietary problems will thoughtfully let me know ahead of time that something does or does not contain my enemy food. If they tell me it is okay for me to eat, then I feel I must take some of it even if it is something I really don't care for. Oh my! What a mess I make for myself.

In searching my past, I try to figure out why I have not outgrown this type of worry. All of my siblings and I were raised with the admonition, "What will the neighbors think?" That may be part of my problem. Actually my geographic neighbors probably don't know or care what I am doing most of the time. We live far enough back from the road that they would have to get really, really nosy to even see what I am doing. As long as no helicopters hover overhead, I am pretty safe from anyone's eyes here at home.

It is the neighbors I invent to worry about that cause my problems. Such as the maid or the woman in New York who probably sent out a dozen letters telling other women they haven't sent in the form yet. Come to think of it, it was a form letter. I'm sure I wasn't singled out as the only culprit.

I have noticed that a lot of women are dressing up more these days than they did a few years back. I see more dresses and less slack suits when I visit offices around the Square. I was so happy when slacks became permissible in almost any setting, and I wish the trend weren't going the other way again. Now that I am not working in an office each day, it shouldn't sadden me. But there are certain places that I go where I am beginning to feel underdressed in slacks. Do you think the other people have noticed that I am not in style?

Back to the hotel maid. At least she knew that I do take baths on occasion. Or do you think she noticed that I took the little bottle of shampoo and the cake of soap?

A HORROR STORY

One of the hidden benefits about having a book published is finding old friends who have heard about the book. This happened to me when a man whom I had dated in my youth wrote to ask for an autographed copy. Of course, I was glad to oblige.

I also instantly had floods of memories about the crowd we used to run with. Since that was wartime, there were not too many guys around except those who were essential to food production. Therefore, we became a rather close-knit group that had lots of fun together at the end of long work days for the farm boys.

Along with these memories, I tried to recall the last time I had seen my friend. I knew he attended our wedding along with his girlfriend from Cottey College who later became his wife. Then I remembered another later time.

My sister Ellen had been recently widowed and was going to summer school away from her house. To help out, I was keeping her three children at our home. We had three children of our own by then. Lester was also attending summer school out of town, so I was taking care of these six children rang-ing in age from two to eleven. In preparation for taking my sister's children home that weekend, I decided to wash and iron (I actually did iron back then!) all of their clothes so she wouldn't be faced with that when she got home. I had all six children wear as few clothes as possible, so that I could wash everything at once.

In preparation for staying a few days with my sister, I decided I needed to mow our lawn. Since three of the children were old enough to help, I made a game with each doing two rounds of our large lawn while I stayed in the house and ironed. My mother came over to help. She and I took turns on that hot day ironing all the clothes of six children and my own duds.

For the first (and last) time ever, I had given myself a home permanent the day before. I wasn't at all skilled at setting hair but wasn't really worried since all I was doing was mowing the lawn (on a windy day) and ironing. The moist, thick grass splattered my legs with green up to the bottoms of my pedal pushers.

To protect my floors, I took off my grassy shoes at the door. I stood barefooted under the torn-down archway in our home, ironing and visiting with my mother.

Before he left for summer school, Lester and I had started remodeling our small house. We had taken out a wall and roughed in an archway before we ran out of time. Since the construction didn't interfere with daily living, we didn't worry about the gaps showing up through the attic. It was summer. Everything else was open.

Out the front window I saw a spiffy-looking

sports car drive in. A man, wearing a suit, got out. Now, no one wore suits in August in Missouri in pre-air-conditioned days. Assuming he was a salesman, I casually went to the door when, to my horror, I saw that it was my boyfriend from fifteen years before.

The kids, all curious about the stranger, ran up in their underpants and shorts to see what was going on. There I stood, barefooted, with green legs, fuzzy hair, six half-naked kids swarming around me, and the unfinished room behind me covered with hangers of freshly ironed clothes hanging from every conceivable spot along with folded clothes on every chair.

After I had the presence of mind to ask him in, he said his wife and children were in the car. Of course, I asked them in also and gasped as they got out. The daughter wore a ruffly dress, socks with lace on the cuffs, and patent leather shoes. The boy had neat shorts with contrasting color shirt and matching socks. I have no idea what his stylish wife was wearing. I think they had been to a funeral or something.

I guess we visited a while. I can't remember. But I can be sure that my friend left thanking his lucky stars that he had been at my wedding as a guest, not having a major role.

WATCH YOUR FRONT DOOR!

Sometimes things happen that I just have to write about. Most of the time it is because I have done something stupid. But if I can't laugh at myself then I don't have the right to laugh at you, so I am going to tell on myself.

A few weeks ago a friend and I were working together to provide an evening meal for another friend who wasn't feeling well. We had the meal all planned out so that each of us provided part of the food for what we hoped would be a nice balanced meal. As both of them lived in town, and I live several miles out in the country, we decided that I could leave my offerings at Susie's house when I was in town earlier for a meeting and Susie (not her real name) would deliver the meal at the proper time.

Susie called me to say that she might not be at home when I brought my food, but she would leave the front door unlocked and I should just go in and put the food in the refrigerator which was in view of the front door. After receiving directions to her house, I prepared the salad and dessert for the meal and went by the street where Susie lives. I remembered her saying that her house was the second one after the turn. I walked up to the door and rang the bell. When no one answered, I opened the unlocked door and started inside with my dishes of food. After about three steps, I was startled to see a young man appear out of an inside room, looking very puzzled at my appearance. I explained that I was bringing this food for Susie to deliver later in the day, and I was supposed to put it in the refrigerator. Looking even more puzzled he replied that no one named Susie lived here. He didn't even live here himself but had dropped by his mother's house for a minute. He wasn't sure where Susie did live but thought she probably lived next door.

I took my dishes and headed down the street to the next house. I knew I was in the right place because the door was unlocked as Susie had said, the refrigerator was in plain view of the front door, and inside the refrigerator there was very little food. Susie had said would be the case when I asked if she would have room to keep the food cool. I put the two dishes inside the refrigerator and went on my merry way.

Later that afternoon, I called the house where our ill friend lived. I explained that I wanted to be sure the food had arrived because Susie wasn't at home when I left my dishes. Our friend assured me that it had not only arrived but had already been consumed by her family and she thanked me for remembering them this way.

End of story? Not quite. This week I saw my partner in the dinner giving and thanked her for delivering the food for us. She said she had been meaning to call me to tell me that when she got home late that afternoon, a neighbor came over asking her if she knew a Carolyn. He came home and found two dishes of food in his refrigerator and a note signed by Carolyn. Though we don't know how he figured it might be intended for Susie, he had the kindness to find out and took the food to her. It seems that Susie did live next door to the young man's mother, but it was on the other side of the house. I entered two homes where no one was expecting me and tried to leave food in their refrigerator. And I never entered the one house where I was supposed to go.

We're grateful that the puzzled man who found food didn't just enjoy it himself thinking maybe there were little elves after all. And I am grateful that the young man who was in his mother's home didn't charge me with breaking and entering. Susie requested that I not use her real name for fear people would find out how many people have unlocked doors in her friendly neighborhood.

The moral of this story is, if you don't keep your doors locked, someday you may come home and find some crazy middle age plus woman has left something you don't really want to deal with. She's not a very good cook anyway!

I STILL HAVE MY WITS

As I go deeper into this age, I find there are some frailties that I freely own up to and others that I keep denying. There is no way I can hide the fact that my memory for names is slipping. It isn't really slipping; it has already gone down that slippery slope.

I was making a long distance call to a dear friend who was in the hospital. It was one of these hospitals where you are connected directly to the room of the patient. I was expecting to have an operator answer and then direct the call to my friend. To my surprise the voice at the other end just weakly said, "Hello." I realized what had happened, but in that instant I lost the name of my friend.

I tried to cover it up by starting to ask how she was feeling, but then realized that if she had a roommate, I might to talking to a stranger. I had an inspiration. I asked if I was indeed speaking to the illustrious past dean of the School of Missions. And I was. I never did remember her real name until an hour or so after the conversation.

If my brain can work quickly enough to cover up such a flaw, why can't it simply give the name I need? I have known this friend for over thirty years, roomed with her at events, traveled across country with her, but I couldn't come up with her name. Now, if any of you know her, please don't tell Margie that her name escaped me.

I dread the greeting time at church because sometimes I need to introduce newcomers to some of us old-timers. Since I fear that I will have trouble with a name somewhere, I usually just pass it over by saying, "Why don't you two introduce yourselves to each other."

When I was a pre-schooler (they didn't call it that then) a rowdy little boy lived next door. He once pushed me into the corner of the front steps and cut my forehead so badly that I had to have stitches in it. I still have the scar if you could see it among all the wrinkles.

This boy's name was Hewitt Griggs Robertson, Jr. We called him Junior. After seventy years, I can still glibly tell you his full name at any time, but I can't remember the name of the lady in our last church who always sat in front of me and had such a sweet expression on her face.

I also have had to let people know that I don't always hear everything exactly as it is said. I hope to remedy that soon with hearing aids, but I can't put them in until a previous procedure has healed fully. I hear what you are saying to me, but I am not always sure if you said "dream" or "scream." It can make quite a difference in the meaning.

This has come on me during the year that I am to record happenings in two of my organizations to report to the paper. Some younger speakers slide over words so quickly that I am afraid I have not recorded them correctly. I might leave out an idea rather than misquote it. People used to speak more distinctly when I was younger.

Some of the 'goodies' that have come with my age are so evident that there is no need to deny them, but I don't like it when anyone thinks that my physical abilities are shot.

I don't need a hand up when I am seated in a soft chair. I just need enough elbow room so that I can push myself up. I can walk faster than most adults. I just prefer to take my time to enjoy my surroundings. When walking up a steep hill, I don't really have to stop for breath. It is more fun to pause a few seconds to look back at the view. And when I am sitting comfortably in a chair in the evening, I don't doze off during the television programs. Since I need some time to think, I block out the program for awhile.

I am middle age plus with some changes in my abilities, but I can still think fast enough to maneuver my way around most embarrassing situations caused by my failings. Just don't ask me to admit them.

HOW TO BE A BORE

Some people seem to think that those of us who are middle age plus spend a lot of our time thinking about the past. This isn't true. We spend a lot of our time trying to remember the present. Who was that lady who spoke to me in the store today? And what did I promise to get done today for the committee I am on? But I have to admit that we can't seem to resist telling stories from the past to people who don't know or care about our experiences.

At a recent luncheon, the women at the table with me were discussing water—Nevada's sulphur water to be exact. Some mentioned having guests who brought bottled water to put in the ice cube trays when they visited. Others discussed the merits of our water compared to our neighboring El Dorado Spring's water. All of this started because one of the women had visited a famous overseas spring where the water was bottled and sold. Although the water in that city tasted fine, she said that bottled spring water tasted just like Nevada's water.

Here's where my years took over. I just had to say that the fact that we had water running out of faucets in our homes was enough for me no matter what the water tasted like. I can remember various times that this luxury was not a reality for us.

In my childhood, we did have a cold water faucet in the house and two outside for washing dirty hands and feet. But the only way we got hot water was by using the tea kettle. Since the tea kettles of my youth were much larger than any you can buy today, one kettle full gave us enough warm water to wash the dishes and rinse them afterwards. (We called it scalding the dishes then.)

In our married life, we have lived several places where we didn't have running water. One place had a faucet in a kitchen sink, but for some reason the homeowner had not completed the drain. We caught the water under the sink in a big bucket which Lester carried out when it got about two-thirds full.

One time, we were hosts to one of those cooking pan salesmen who cooked a meal in the home to sell those wonderful pans that made the food taste so good. The salesman/cook kept running water to put in the pans and draining excess juices from the food while we kept hearing the sound of the water in the bucket getting higher and higher. We were too proud to tell him the problem, and thankfully he finished his demonstration before water spilled out on the floor. The bucket was so full Lester had to ladle some out before he could carry it out to empty it. We didn't buy any of the pans either.

Another time when we had both a baby and a preschool child, we lived in a modern house in the country with kitchen, bath, and utility room all well-equipped with faucets, sinks, drains, and tubs. But the well went dry. For one long, hot summer we had to haul water in ten gallon milk cans from town for our daily supply. This was before the days of laundromats and disposable diapers. We had to save the wash water to flush the toilet, mop the floors, and water the few flowers that survived that hot summer.

Since my listeners' eyes became somewhat glazed over and the business of the meeting was about to begin, I couldn't tell all of these experiences at the table, but I think everyone got the point. Nevada has good water because it is plentiful, safe to drink, and now, I think it taste good. In fact, I didn't mind the 'old' water because it tasted like home. We were always so glad to get back home each summer that driving west on Austin Street and smelling the sulphur in the air was a good welcome for our family.

I'm wondering, the next time our group meets for our regular luncheon meetings, if any of these ladies will be brave enough to sit at the same table with me again. They probably will be afraid that I will have another story from the past.

Whatever subject comes up, I am sure I could add my two-cents worth. In the meantime, did I ever tell you about the time that....

FRIGID IN AUGUST

When I think of my childhood summers, I remember hot, dry Augusts where the grass crinkled under my bare feet, dusty roads led to friends' homes where lawns had been picked bare by chickens, and water pans for pets and fowl soon went dry. One vivid memory I shared with my father as we drove to town in our old green Buick when the temperature reached 115 degrees. It was so hot that my father actually unbuttoned the top two buttons on his dress shirt instead of the usual one when he was in 'casual attire.' The steering wheel of the car was too hot to touch with bare hands, so Papa took out his folded white handkerchief to use as a hot pad. Of course there was no air-conditioning in the car, and the hot wind blew in all four of the opened windows as we drove home to seek the sanctuary of the shade of the stately elm trees in the lawn. I was excited to go to town with my father and don't remember feeling much discomfort from the heat.

We ate in the dining room that was on the north side of the house so, therefore, didn't receive the southwest breeze that the living room enjoyed. However, we never considered taking our plates elsewhere to eat. We ate in the dining room. The kitchen was also fairly warm during the summer and we rarely had a meal that didn't require some cooking. Our bedrooms were upstairs where the heat would rise during the day, though at night there was usually a nice breeze in two of the rooms. The 'girls' north room and the 'boys' northwest rooms were not as favored but we managed to sleep through the night. Some of our neighbors put up a bedstead in their lawn to use on the hottest nights. The only time we slept outside was for adventure, not to escape the heat.

During the 1930s we continued our summertime activities fairly much as in any other month except that we kept the windows open and spent leisure times outside in the shade. Summers were meant to be hot. We coped with the heat and still enjoyed life.

This summer I spent much of my time, even on days that reached into the 90s, wearing a jacket or keeping a blanket over my feet and legs. While I was in the hospital where my husband was a patient, I sometimes swiped one of his bed blankets to wrap in because the room was so cold. In the car I had to be careful to keep the cold air from blowing from the air-conditioner right into my face because it tended to cause me to have cold symptoms.

I was a teacher at a denominational study at a United Methodist college in Arkansas where we slept in the dormitories. I was so cold the first night there that I had to sleep in my robe and slippers with a heavy blanket over me. And I was still cold. In the morning, I discovered how to turn the air off completely. For the rest of the week, I had a fairly comfortable room, still a little cold from air seeping in from the halls and neighboring rooms. I used only the blanket and left my robe hanging for the cold trips in the middle of the night down the hall to the restroom.

Since my classroom's temperature was controlled by computer in some office far away, we learned to come to class with wraps. I gave frequent breaks so the students could move around to warm up a bit.

At the end of the week, I looked forward to coming home to an environment where money was not being wasted to make the inhabitants too cold for comfort. Then I spent a thirteen hour day as a judge at the primary election. I was assigned to Ward 1 in the Community Center. When we arrived at 5:30 a.m., it was raining, so we came in slightly damp to a room that registered 68 degrees on the computer controlled thermostat. As soon as we finished our duties of arranging the room, we each became very chilly. Soon I passed the chilly mark and was downright cold. During a break, I asked the staff if they could adjust the temperature higher, but they were helpless to make the change. It had to be done somewhere else. After another cold hour, we called City Hall to complain and learned that it was controlled by the store that installed the system. We thought they might make adjustments but none came. We finally had the door to the hall opened to let in some of the outside air. Though that made us more comfortable, it bothered my scotch ancestry to pay money to cool the building the same time we were letting in hot air to make it livable.

So are we experiencing progress? In the 1930s, we were hot when the temperature was hot. Seventy years later we are too cold when the temperature is hot. Somehow that doesn't seem healthy, and I know it isn't cheap. The season will soon be over, and this winter when the room temperature is 68 degrees, we will turn up the thermostat to get warmer. Won't that be nice!

ARM CHAIR GYMNASTICS

I have been quite tired lately because of the Olympics. Trying to keep up with all the events and 'helping' the participants with my body language and tensions have sapped my strength. I should have worked harder at getting into condition before the day arrived. You see, my goal is to experience the Gold Medal at the Olympics on Route One, Nevada, Missouri.

At this event, which is not highly publicized, I admit, I have been a contender for years, but have never achieved the Gold. I thought I was doing quite well with the 'trip-a-to and sull' event in the ice skating, until I found out that I was not pronouncing the words correctly. I had been doing nicely tripping over my own feet, and I certainly became quite sullen after such an episode. I kept hearing about how hard it was to land these movements correctly. When arising from a chair, I usually have to take only one little extra step to land the movement, and I rarely fall down at such a time. But it was pointed out to me that the term was "triple-toe axle." When I watched a little closer, I could see that I wasn't coming close to the required motions, and besides, I always had on too many clothes for those events.

It puzzles me that if ice skating or ice dancing is to show the beauty of the human body in motion, then why is it that the female human body is nearly bare, while the male is covered from ankles to neck with maybe only occasionally a couple of unbuttoned shirt buttons? I was not in the fashion mode of these events. I had to look elsewhere for my opportunities.

It looked like The Luge might be a better possibility. In that competition all I had to do was lie on my back perfectly still and let the sled carry me quickly down a slippery slope. As a child I was an avid sledder. I could run and belly-flop on a sled that carried me down a hill to the closed-off street for a one-block coast to our house. When there were more children than sleds, I plopped on top of one or two other kids on the same sled that went even faster down the same track. My older brothers even allowed me to top off their personnel on a sled if there weren't too many other people watching.

With that background, The Luge should be a snap for me. My only trouble is that I have to see where I am going. If I keep popping my head up to watch the world go by, my teammates would never choose me as a partner. I had enough problems as the youngest in the family, always being chosen last when we divided into teams for games. I didn't want to risk that again at my middle age plus age, so I gave up my chance for the Gold in The Luge.

I have had some terrific dreams where I was flying, so ski jumping sounds like a natural. As the skiers soar through the air, they are actually in flight. But the last time we had ice, I took a little flight off the step of our deck and didn't land very gracefully. As television cameras would watch me at the Olympics, and I didn't want to embarrass my children with an awkward landing, I by-passed ski jumping, also.

Cross country skiing or skiing and shooting a gun at the same time appeared to be too much work. I didn't consider those events.

That eliminated almost everything except the commentary. Television personalities don't compete for medals. They compete for ratings. When they have wrung out and hung out to dry the tenth sad story during the long waits for the weather to cooperate, I felt that these people really did deserve some recognition. A detailed story of the inside workings of a make-shift studio whose event was put on hold should be rated right up there with the pulled groin and the flu bug. But it seems that those of us who compete with words don't get much recognition, even if we're up against a deadline or trying to fill space.

Therefore, this won't be the year that I medal at the Olympics. I won't even get a Silver or a Bronze. But I have a Bronze pond outside my home, a Silver moon in my bedroom window at night, and a large flock of Golden finches at my feeder. My armchair gymnastics have given me something to brag about.

Now with a few more days of rest, I will be as good as new again. (Well, as good as middle age plus ever gets, anyway!)

A TIME TO KEEP

Among my souvenirs are things
I'll never need
Comfort, style, and sentiment are
synonyms for greed

NO TIME FOR TIME SAVING

I have been very busy lately because we have, through the years, acquired many time-saving pieces of equipment. This year we bought a different, larger, better-equipped, riding mower. It can cut a wider swath than our old one. It doesn't require shifting to change directions, and it has power steering. It is easy to use and cuts so well that we have increased the amount of grass that we mow. I now mow behind the windbreak, around all the farm buildings, and anywhere else I think would look better with short grass. It used to take me about three hours to mow the lawn with the old mower. With this time-saving new mower, I now spend four hours mowing.

I don't have a bread-making machine, but some friends report that they now make bread daily instead of just for a treat on special occasions. Though it makes better eating, it certainly doesn't save any time.

When I was a child, each of us in our large family used one wash cloth and one towel all week. We had a towel rack for each family member where we kept our personal towel and wash cloth. Recently when we had a house full of company for three days, it seemed that all I did was wash towels. They were not gathered from towel racks but from the bathroom floor, from the deck, and from bedrooms. Because it is so easy to wash and dry towels, we now use clean towels constantly. We don't need to keep our own towels identified and separate because we can just throw them all in the washer and start over with clean ones. Our time-saving laundry equipment runs often and keeps me running also.

Our car is comfortable and cool. Since it is no trouble to jump into the car and run to town for something I need, I do it often. We used to spend time making lists to be sure that we got everything we needed when we went to town. Now if we forget something, it is no big deal. We just run back into town to get it. We use many hours this way, but we are comfortable and cool.

This computer that I am using to write saves many hours of work. It alphabetizes a list in seconds; it brings up an article I wrote a year ago for me to check a fact or remember what I said. It keeps records, helps investigate information for genealogy, and allows me to play games with competition all by myself. Because it is so convenient, I find more and more that I can do with it what I wouldn't have done in the past. So I save time while adding things to do that take more time.

Washing dishes is fairly easy now. We don't have a dishwasher in our home today but have had them in some houses in the past. It was easy to rinse the dishes off, put them into the dishwasher, and wait until I had a full load to run the dishwasher. We used lots of dishes because it was so easy to get them clean. If a bigger dish worked better than the one I had already started to use, it was no problem. I simply got the bigger one and started over. It didn't matter that I dirtied another dish. Even now, when I don't have a dishwasher, with the new detergents, running hot water, a rinsing hose, double sink, and a dish drain, dishwashing is not a chore to dread.

I could write about more time-saving equipment, such as the tools my husband uses and housecleaning helps that I have. But I'm afraid I don't have time. I have to run back to town to get gas for the lawn tractor to mow the area behind the pond bank. No one can see it, but it would look so nice if it were mowed.

DOT COM

We enjoyed a short visit from my sister who had recently purchased a new computer. This machine had all the extras including a fax, scanner, possibilities for e-mail, access to the Internet and anything else you can think of. However, she has not mastered all the ins and outs of this monster. Since my husband has a similar, but not as elaborate set-up, they spent a good deal of time during her visit talking about computer problems. Phrases like, byte, Windows, mouse, and margins, were used in ways completely different from the meaning I give to those words. In talking about all the advantages these programs gave them, they also kept worrying about all the problems they were running into while learning the new systems.

Ellen said she had to leave her house (and the computer) to walk around the block several times to relax after trying to master some of the new advances. Though she came to visit us to get away from the stress for a few days, she and Lester continued to share frustrations.

While listening to their talk, I created this paraphrase for the old poem, "A Horseshoe Nail."

For want of a dot com a program was lost
For want of a program a contract was lost.
For want of a contract a business was lost.
For want of a business a fortune was lost.
All for the want of a stupid dot com!

Although both of these computer hacks share the joys of being middle age plus with me, they have become much more interested in this new world of communication than I.

I use a word processor to write my columns and articles, but that is not much different from using my electronic typewriter. Even with this narrow use of a computer, I occasionally run into problems frustrating to me that are easily solved by someone who knows what to do.

I wonder if our parents found some of the same problems when they adopted more modern communications such as the dial phone. I remember an operator calling and instructing us in the use of the dial. She asked us to dial a number to be sure we were fully informed. Now dial phones themselves are becoming rare. We punch numbers. If we don't have a touch tone phone, we are left hanging on the line at many businesses that tell us to punch 1 for this and 2 for that.

Even while celebrating that I can carry a phone outside and not be worried about missing a call, I still find myself longing for the days when we actually spoke to people, not machines.

When Ellen left, she said, "Now you don't have to call me. Just use my e-mail!" That doesn't let me hear her voice, and I can't be sure she gets the message. Anyway, I probably couldn't get to the computer to send the message without pushing Lester away first! I think I will still punch in her number on the phone!

INSTRUCTIONS INCLUDED

We are now driving a new car. This car has several options on it that I wasn't used to in our little economy cars of the past. To be prepared to drive this vehicle, I spent a whole evening reading the instruction booklet from cover to cover. I didn't read about the parts and where they go and all that stuff, but I mastered all the techniques of aligning the seats, taking care of the lights, and using the cruise control, which was a little different from what I was used to. I read all the dials on the instrument panel so that I would know when something was wrong. I even learned how to set the radio for my two favorite stations and how to reset the clock when daylight savings comes on.

I felt that I was a well-prepared operator of our new car, and I had no hesitation about driving out into the real world in all our glory. Our great-granddaughter was with me in the back seat to avoid the danger of the air bag in case of a little fender bender. As we were driving down Austin Street, she spied a friend in another car and called out to me over the CD player that was playing Lawrence Welk's polkas, "Grandmommy, there's Bill. Honk so he will see us in the new car." Obligingly, I pressed on the center of the steering wheel. Nothing happened. I had learned how to do everything in this modern car except the one thing that was the same in all the cars I had driven since I was eleven years old. I pressed again with no results. By then our friend had passed without the pleasure of waving to Marilyn. When I got home, I looked at the steering wheel more carefully and saw two little horn symbols imbedded in the material that hides the air bag. When pressed, the horn will sound.

I realized that you are never really prepared until you have actually completed the action. And sometimes the least complicated thing can be what causes the problem. A simple push with my thumb on the right spot was all that was needed. I hadn't read about that in the book, or if I had, I thought it was so simple I didn't bother to remember it.

We used to have a VCR that had two buttons on it. We could insert a tape, put the television control on Channel 3, press play, and be in business. After several years, it started acting up. We got a new one, a better one. This machine has all sorts of things to push and record. It even has words coming on the screen where 12:00 used to flash on our old one. It tells us "Hi," and it tells us "Bye." If operated right, I am told, it will tell us "Play," but I have so much trouble getting all the buttons synchronized that I often give up, deciding I don't want to see the tape after all. Then I have the problem of getting it to tell me "Bye" and let me go back to watching a program on televison. I find the instruction booklet to figure it out and finally get back to a show which is now half way through. I yearn for my old simple VCR that didn't talk to me, or do anything but record and play my tapes when I punched one of the two buttons.

We have a remote for this VCR which sits in a row with the remotes for the television, the stereo, and the satellite dish. Each of these appliances needs its own contraption for starting and stopping, as well as choosing what station, CD, or channel we want to enjoy. Although we can control everything without rising from the lounge chair, my frustration level uses as much energy as getting up to go to the machine. First I must find a little flashlight to read all the small letters on the black background if I do operate it by hand.

I don't want to go back to our old Edison phonograph that required winding between records or the older cars that you had to start with a crank, but sometimes I think my brain can't handle any more memory buttons to push.

If you can operate it, honk if you agree with me!

A MOVING EXPERIENCE

Have you had a moving experience lately? Although it has been several years since our last move (and I fervently hope it will be our last one), it is still a clear memory.

This memory is revived when any of our children move to a new home. When Susan and Mark were moving, she coined the phrase "domestic archeology" to describe the *stuff* we always find when we begin digging into closets and shelves to box things up for the move. On top we see the current history of our lives. As we dig deeper, we find reminders of an earlier period, and at the very bottom are remnants of our own ancient history.

Since our marriage has included college years, army moves, and changes of professions, ending with being a parsonage family, we have moved sixteen times. Our first move used the back seat of our car. The last move took the largest U-Haul, three pickup trucks, and two cars. There are still three barrels of *stuff* stored in the family granary that we have not unpacked. I can't remember now what layers of domestic archeology those barrels contain. If we haven't needed them in several years, probably they aren't too crucial. But I will guarantee that when I do get into them, I will probably not be able to part with much.

I sometimes envy folk who have lived in the same house for years. They have never had to go through those wrenching decisions about what to keep and what to throw out. But pity their poor children who will someday have to face all that *stuff* after the parents make their final move. That is the saddest type of moving—when you must arrange for possessions of a loved one who is no longer there. Though that has happened to us, it still doesn't spur us to get rid of our own *stuff*. We can pass some responsibilities on to the next generation.

March used to be the month to move because farmers could put in a garden and plant the crops. Now it seems that moving time is more often at the end of a school year. We sometimes had trouble contracting a moving van in June when it was time for ministers in our denomination to move.

There is a certain day for United Methodist ministers to move. Because there has to be an empty parsonage to move into, everyone must move at once. This arrangement can get very tricky when one moving company is a little slow and another faster. We have moved out the front door while the next family was moving in the back. Some of the new family's *stuff* almost got moved on with our *stuff*. Kids and pets complicate this process, as the new kids, in their excitement to see their next home, open doors that release pets that had been shut up for the move.

I am glad to be permanently back home and to let my memories of moving carry me for the rest of my life. My current theme song is, "Like a tree that's planted by the water, we shall not be moved."

SPRING CLEANING

Hearing the words, "This is the first day of spring," makes each of us feel younger and peppier. Even the ogre of spring cleaning can't dampen our spirits. However those of us who are middle age plus remember when spring cleaning was a very big event, involving the whole family, whether they wanted to help or not.

One of the biggest hurdles of this routine was taking down the heating stove. No matter how careful we were, we couldn't take the stove pipes from the stove and out of the ceiling or wall without spreading soot over the whole house. Always a nice collection of the sooty stuff waited to spring at us as we pulled out the last section of pipe. After cleaning up the mess, we carted the stove off to the garage or back porch to allow more space in the living room for summer activities. Then we put the little round asbestos or metal covering over the hole to the chimney and forgot about firing up the stove until next fall.

However, when next fall came, the stove pipes never fit together in the right way, even though they came from the same stove and the same wall. Something was always different enough to make the fittings not work.

Another hazard of this spring ritual with the heating stove was taking the stove down too early. After a few warm days of spring, we would get anxious to get the process over with and rush to get the stove out of the room. Invariably the next day it cooled off or turned into blackberry winter when we would freeze for days. We wouldn't dream of putting the stove back up again. We'd sit around the oven of the cook stove or savor the heat from the sun in a sheltered spot outside until the real warm weather finally arrived.

I have said that the test of a strong marriage is whether a couple could take down and put up a stove together. (Another good test is laying a piece of linoleum that has been measured to fit exactly in a certain area.)

After taking the stove down, many people removed their winter rug and replaced it with a more summery floor covering. If they were lucky enough to have good wooden floors, they left the floors bare in the summer.

I don't ever remember not having a vacuum sweeper, but I have seen others draping a big room-sized rug over the clothesline and beating it with oval-shaped metal beaters about the size of a tennis racket. Clouds of dust arose from each whack on the rug. Probably most of it found its way back down on the rug again when the dust settled.

Now all we have to do when spring comes is flick the control button on the thermostat from heat to cool. With no fuss or bother, our furnace will change from heating us warmly to cooling us. Though it makes the need for spring cleaning much less urgent, most of us feel a little guilty unless we make some pretense of a deep cleaning each spring. I plan to start mine very soon. I have definite plans to start my cleaning for last year as soon as I get organized.

OUR NEW CARPET

I often talk about how great it is to live in a smaller community where people know you and call you by name. However, this last month I found some drawbacks to that situation. When workmen come to my house, sometimes I'm happier if they don't know anything about me.

Since we were adding to our house, we decided to put new carpet over the whole house. We thought it'd be great to have a fresh look everywhere until we realized it meant moving everything. In our small house there aren't many spots to move rooms full of furniture into. Actually, the furniture itself isn't as big a problem as the *stuff* that we have on and under it. All those precious pictures of grandchildren and great-grandchildren have to be put someplace where we weren't going to lay carpet. Where could that be? The bathrooms!

After we had both tubs full of pictures, books, items from our desks, and little objects such as waste baskets and suitcases, we started using the floor. Obviously, at least one bathroom had to have a path left inside for essential purposes. Everything else was filled.

Then came the really fun part—moving the furniture. Though the nice man from the store was equipped to do this, and Lester was handy to help, I had to keep running ahead, or behind, to catch all the tell-tale dust they uncovered. Can you picture the amount of dust that accumulates on bed slats when you had carpenters working in the house for several weeks? (I was thankful that we had the excuse of the workmen's sawdust because there probably would have been just as much dust, even if we hadn't been remodeling!)

Naturally, since we were planning on new carpet, I had not vacuumed the old one in recent days. This neglect left the opportunity to discover little treasures as we shifted each piece of furniture to a new position. Some things I had forgotten we owned appeared. I found some I had been looking for for days.

Since the whole process took two long days and the carpenters were also still working on their projects in other rooms, I started recklessly putting things wherever I could find an empty spot. An open drawer became a depository for items never intended for drawers. My Endust can emptied as I frantically wiped every cleared spot I found. The kitchen table was loaded, except for one little corner spot for our plates and glasses. Even the one narrow path in the bathroom was filled as space for furniture ran out.

When the beautiful carpet was completely installed, we took a few moments to admire the effect before moving everything back. It's funny how easy it is to forget just exactly where each piece fit when in tight quarters. We eventually moved everything to the proper place in time for the carpet layer to go home. Then we had to remove all that *stuff* from the table and out of the bathrooms. (After all, it had been two days since we could take a bath!) What we formerly kept on the floor or under the bed looked too tacky to put on our new carpet. Since we rearranged the furniture slightly in this process, some of the *stuff* lost its parking place and some just didn't look right any more.

Actually a miracle had happened in those bathrooms during those two days. What we stashed there grew until we had much more *stuff* to put away then we had originally. I still have a drawer full of items that should go on a desk. My closets are jammed full. But the floors look great!

Not once did the carpet layer make an unkind remark about our *stuff*. I don't know how well he knew us before he came, but I know that now he knows us far better than he ever wanted to. I probably will run into him in town some day, but maybe he won't recognize me without a dust rag in my hand and a frantic look on my face. I'll sure know him, though.

TOURIST CABINS WITH OUTHOUSES

I have been traveling quite a bit lately. I love to travel by car because I feel that I am in control. I can stop and start when I please without worrying about making connections in big airports or sitting in a hot plane while waiting for weather to clear somewhere.

I grew up taking a three-day trip twice each year, back and forth from Washington, D.C. to Nevada, Missouri. I'm sure my mother did not cherish those trips, but she would put up with anything to get back to her beloved Wayside near Nevada.

My memories of those trips are mainly good. I enjoyed eating out at all the interesting places along the way and staying in hotels. What I didn't like was staying in what was called tourist cabins. Since my mother was more frugal than my father, when she was herding our brood across the country without him, we usually stayed at these less-expensive tourist cabins.

For one dollar a night, we could rent one cabin that had a bed or two and one light hanging in the middle of the room. The room had no ceiling or plaster. We saw just the back of the wooden siding and exposed rafters. In the yard outside was a hand pump and down a path an outhouse. We all hated staying in those cabins. I think one reason my mother used these facilities was that they were right beside the highway. We didn't have to drive into the cities to find a hotel.

When my father was along, we always headed right into the center of town for a hotel. The elevators, long carpeted halls, and large rooms with a private bath were great fun for me. Occasionally the hotel didn't have a private bath, and we had to go down the hall to share a bath with other travelers. But still, it was better than the outhouses at the tourist cabins.

Restaurants were a big treat, also. In those days the highways usually went right down main street, and the restaurants were all in the middle of town. We each took a turn at selecting the place we would eat. No one could object. My siblings dreaded when it was my choice, as I dearly loved the ones with red checkered tablecloths. I now call them greasy spoon cafes, but then I thought they were great.

When I drive to Springfield today on Historic U.S. 66, I see the remains of gas stations, cafes, and tourist camps of the type I grew up with. It brings back pleasant memories. But I drive happily into a nearby McDonalds to use their clean restrooms and enjoy their predictable menu. I watch for signs of a Super 8 Motel or another reliable chain and let my memories of past travels rest while I enjoy the present conveniences of automobile travel.

I REALLY MISS BARNS

I miss barns. Oh, I know there are many buildings, sheds, and garages on every farm, but I miss
those big old barns that used to proclaim to the world
that this farm was one of distinction.

Such barns are not appropriate today because the
need for haylofts is gone. Farmers leave the hay in
the field in huge round bales, saving time, labor, and
building upkeep. Shelter for farm animals is often
provided out in the pasture with sheds open on one
side. Dairy barns are laboratories with gleaming fix-
tures, tubes, and metal barriers.

The days of wooden stalls with straw scattered
on the floor and wooden feeding boxes arranged on
either side of a walkway with a ladder leading up to
the hayloft are gone.

I have always loved exploring or playing in the
old-style barns. Even in my childhood winters in Washington, D.C., there was a huge old barn not too far
from our home. This building resembled the present-
day split-level houses. The farmer could enter the
hayloft from the top of a hill through a large door that
easily swung open for a good-sized wagon. He entered
the lower floor of the barn from the bottom of the hill.

There was the area that provided space for stalls, animals, feed, and storage. Since this barn was no longer used, my friends and I spent many happy hours using it as headquarters for various imaginative games.

The barn on my grandfather's farm here in Vernon County was not as grand, but it did have the large loft, the typical barn roof, and the stalls, walkways and feeding boxes necessary to care for a variety of animals. The barn still stands, but without the hayloft which gave it character.

In my memory we did not use our own barn for animals, but we did have a wonderful hayloft until one day in the 1950s when my father decided to streamline the building by removing the loft and making the building a machine shed. I was heartbroken. I now realize the economy of his decision since we had no need to store hay.

Whenever I go to the Schell City Wildlife Refuge, I drool over the huge barn and silo that stand neglected and fenced away from the public on the south side of one of the largest lakes. I'd love to enter the wide corridor and let my imagination provide animals for each of the many stalls that line the building. When I run out of projects to work on, I think I will start a drive to have the barn restored as an historic learning spot for children. We restore old schoolhouse for the modern child to know what their ancestors' schools were like. Barns are also a part of our heritage. Children will profit from time spent inside a great old barn.

I really miss barns.

FOOD WRAPS

I ran out of plastic wrap today when I needed to cover a cake I was taking to a dinner. I began searching for alternatives to keep the cake clean and fresh. Waxed paper with scotch tape holding it in place did the job. This chore reminded me about the first time I ever heard of, or saw, plastic wrap.

I was attending a demonstration meeting in an Extension Club in Webster County, Missouri, where we lived. The Home Demonstration Agent, as she was called then, was showing us new items coming on the market. She wrapped a bowl of potato salad in plastic wrap and then turned the bowl upside down. We were all amazed that the salad didn't fall immediately to the floor.

When I was a child, my mother always wrapped my two sandwiches and a cookie in waxed paper before putting them in a brown paper bag to carry to school. This waxed paper was very helpful during recess to catch and keep the tadpoles I found in a playground puddle or to fold into various designs when weather discouraged outdoor fun at noon recess. Though I took waxed paper for granted, my mother occasionally remarked how nice it was to have this product.

Earlier she sent school lunches for my siblings in a lard bucket or a lunch pail with a tight lid without wrapping the food.

When she took a dish to a community dinner or to a club, she put it in a basket with a tea towel across the top. She hailed the convenience of waxed paper with the same enthusiasm as I greeted the plastic wrap in the early 1950s and aluminum foil which was introduced after World War II. Both inventions made a difference in our kitchens.

When we were children we used to think tinfoil from chewing gum and celluloid dolls were great. Our own children grew up with plastic in every aspect of their lives. Since these man-made materials, though helpful, do not decompose like paper, we have all had to learn how to recycle it to save our environment.

Reusable lunch pails, biodegradable waxed paper, and cloth tea towels weren't real handy, but they didn't remain to spoil the landscape for the next generation of consumers. However, I probably will still buy another roll of plastic wrap the next time I go to town!

PASS THE SALT

I am really enjoying the melons and tomatoes fresh from the garden at this time of year. Of course, they are fresh from someone else's garden since we didn't get a garden put out this year. But with generous offerings on the sharing table at church, the Farmer's Market, and good neighbors, we usually get many good tastes of my favorites.

One drawback appears, however. I like a little salt on cantaloup, watermelon, and tomatoes. Lester says salt ruins the natural good taste, and we know that people who are middle age plus should avoid salt whenever possible. But these vegetables taste so much better with just a little salt.

Over one of our 'friendly' conversations about this matter, we remembered a time when service men, athletes, and others who were working outdoors were routinely supplied with salt tablets to replenish the salt lost through perspiration. Salt was supposed to be good for your body and keep you from becoming light headed or have other dire problems. I never actually took such a tablet, but I remember once when we were visiting the Washington Monument that the Ranger in charge gave my niece a tablet because her face got red when she raced our son, Mark, down all the flights of stairs. Since Ruth had a ruddy complexion, we weren't concerned about the coloring that alarmed the Ranger. I'm not sure if she actually took the tablet or not, but I remember we all lined up at the drinking fountain. The water was probably much more important than the salt.

I wonder if any tests have been made to see if those who did take salt tablets back in those days have a greater incidence of high blood pressure or strokes.

One use of salt I cherished as a child was to sprinkle salt on a little chip of ice from the big block in the icebox. Or if a piece broke off as Riley Kafer carried it into the kitchen from his truck, we kids scrambled for it, covered it with salt from the shaker, and sucked on it until the ice melted. Rock salt used for making ice cream was another treat, especially if it was combined with a little of the crushed ice in the freezer. I recently saw some rock salt scattered on the ground at a parking lot where someone had broken a bag while going to the car. It took all of my will power to keep from picking up a few pieces to take home, rinse off, and enjoy in solitude. I refrained, afraid of what others might think if they saw me.

I ate a meal recently with a woman who sprinkled salt liberally over her entire plate of food before she even tasted anything. The plate had a Waldorf salad on it which I assume would not taste good when salted. Since she was a little on the heavy side, I wondered about her blood pressure. I politely made no comment.

I am in good company when I admit to my preference for a little salt on my vegetables. The Bible speaks warmly about the virtues of salt. We put salt blocks in the fields for livestock or deer to lick.

My father used to keep me busy in the evenings trying to put salt on a wild rabbit's tail as it hopped around the fringes of our lawn. I honestly believed him when he said if I sprinkled some on its tail, I could catch the rabbit. He also used this suggestion when robins hopped nearby. I spent many evenings with a salt shaker in my hand until my mother took pity on me and straightened out my thinking.

It sounds as if I was pretty stupid as a child, but you have to realize that my father was an authority on everything. If he said it, it was so. I have since learned he wasn't always correct, and I learned fairly early that he loved to tease. I gradually learned to distinguish when it was the truth.

My blood pressure is very good, thankfully, and I do not like the liberal use of pepper some have started using to replace salt. Since onions and garlic don't agree with me, for seasoning I stick to my one favorite. As long as Morton's little girl with the umbrella keeps proving that when it rains it pours, I will continue to sprinkle some each day.

HATS OFF!

While doing research on U.S. presidents, I noticed how the styles of men's hats have changed through the years. The formal top hats worn at inauguration ceremonies have been discarded by some of the more recent leaders. Going bareheaded seemed to be a mark of strong, virile men who scorned wearing any headgear.

My father had two main styles of hats. In winter, he wore a gray felt hat with a groove down the center top and a brim of about one and a half inches beneath a sedate gray band. In summer, he wore a white straw hat of the same shape, but the band might have had just a small amount of color on it. He changed from one fabric to the other on September 15 and May 15 each year. In summer, when he was working on the farm, he wore a typical straw farmer's hat. I never saw him wearing anything resembling a cap until his later years when he cherished a warm felt cap with ear flaps that pulled down. This cap, which my sister Miriam gave him, was one of his things that I kept after his death.

In my college years when I first met Lester, he didn't wear any hat at all until in the army when he had to wear the uniform hat. After his discharge, when we were buying civilian clothes, we bought one dress hat which he seldom wore. He now has quite a collection of caps similar to ball caps, but around home he wears a denim work hat in the winter and a lightweight pith-helmet type hat in the summer. A couple of seldom-worn furry hats and caps are in his closet.

The etiquette about wearing hats has also changed. In my childhood, I remember men removing their hats when they entered a house, an elevator, or a restaurant. Last weekend when we were eating in a nice new restaurant, I counted four men wearing caps while they were eating. One young man was definitely on a date. He was holding hands with a woman across the table, but he still had on a tan cap pulled down low over his eyes. Another diner was middle aged, and definitely not on a date. His partner handed him the check when it came. The others were in between the ages of these first two. One man wore a nice white cap into the restaurant, but took it off as he was seated, placing it on the plants near his table.

Many older men like to wear hats because they need the warmth on their bare heads. Others enjoy the protection from the sun. A hat also gives them something to do while talking. They can take it off and put it back on a time or two during a conversation as a sort of punctuation to their words.

There is no stigma against wearing a cap that carries advertisement for a business. Even famous name brands place their trademark or name right above the visor. We used to laugh at Minnie Pearl for letting the tag of her hat show. Now brands are sewn securely in place, in full view. It is a part of the stylishness of the hat.

Since scientists tell us we lose a great deal of our

body warmth through our heads, the practice of wearing hats in cold weather makes good sense. And since scientists also tell us that continued exposure to the sun's rays is dangerous to our skin, so wearing hats in the summer is smart. But what about the ears that stick out in the cold and in the sun under these caps? I would think these appendages would be either frostbitten or sunburned most of the time. I foresee a generation of future middle age plus men with skin problems on their ears wearing wide-brimmed hats too late.

I also foresee that these men will remove these wide-brimmed hats when they enter a house, elevator, or restaurant because they will take up too much room to leave on their heads. And for that I say, "Hats off to them!"

WATER, WATER, EVERYWHERE

Our county has had a lot of water on the brain recently. Rains that would not stop, rivers that didn't end at their banks, ponds that grew and grew, and roads that decided to go swimming bring back lots of memories.

All this water reminded me how we have changed in our personal habits about water. When I was a child, the common practice in the country was to have a water pail sitting on the wash stand with a dipper floating in it. When people wanted a drink, they dipped some water with the dipper, drank it, and, if there was still some water left in the dipper, it either went back into the bucket or into the wash basin beside the bucket. This wash basin then was ready and handy for washing hands before meals. Next to the wash stand was a slop bucket where we dumped the waste water after several had washed their hands in the basin. This water was combined with the scraps from dinner and fed to the pigs later in the day.

We shudder in horror now as we think of all the germs transferred. Everyone drank from the same dipper. We washed our hands in water that had been in or near the lips of other people. Waste water sat in an opened container in the same room where we cooked and ate! How did we ever survive?

But today, with all our emphasis on germs and sanitation, what did we see floating in our recent flood waters? Millions of Styrofoam cups and aluminum cans. Surely that can't be better for humankind than a few family-shared germs.

Our sanitary method of drinking has created new and different problems. We use individual cups, but then what happens? Even when we put them in a waste can, the landfill can't contain them all. As we witnessed in the recent flood, millions were thrown by the roadside.

But, back to our family's drinking water. Remember how excited we were when we had an icebox with a reservoir for drinking water next to the ice compartment? A little spigot at the bottom of the reservoir allowed us to get a cold drink without chipping any ice or opening any door. It took several years for makers of refrigerators to incorporate that simple plan in the electric 'iceboxes' that replaced the ones the iceman filled for us three times a week.

At The Neighbors Center where I worked, we were thrilled to have a refrigerator that had an outside dispenser for ice and for cold water. Often when I placed my glass under the handy lever, I remembered with fondness that old icebox in the family kitchen at home—and, of course, sitting on top of the icebox, the one drinking glass we all shared!

Tonight when I wash the six or eight glasses that accumulate each day as our family and guests ease their thirst, I will praise my hot water heater, my double sink, and the drain that carries waste water far away from our kitchen. And I will also praise my parents for managing to raise a healthy family and live to a ripe old age in spite of ignorance of little things called germs.

Excuse me for a minute. I seem to be very thirsty.

MONDAY, WASH DAY...

Do you remember the little jingle we used to sing, "Today is Monday. Monday washday..."? I was thinking about that last night when I threw a pair of sweaty, dirty jeans in the washer at ten because we didn't want them messing up the place.

In the not too distant past, no one ever planned a meeting for women on Monday because that was the day we all did our laundry. Then on Tuesday, we ironed and ironed and ironed. Today I avoid buying anything that has to be ironed. If I do get something by mistake, I use a can of spray starch, lay a towel on the table, and hook up the iron to spend five minutes pressing the blouse or shirt.

My generation remembers a different type of washday. Not the black boiler in the yard with a fire built under it, though I heard my mother talking about it enough to feel I remember it. The earliest washing machine I do remember was a manual one. It had a wooden handle attached to paddles that someone (usually the older children) pushed back and forth to agitate the water and clothes inside the tank until the human machine wore out or until the mother decided the clothes were clean. Next the clothes were run through a hand-powered wringer into a tub of clean water to be hand rinsed before swinging the wringer around again to transfer the clothes from the first rinse tub into the second. A third wringing action moved the clothes from the second rinse water into the laundry basket.

Later washing machines utilized gas-powered engines, and, finally after rural electrification cooperatives became common, electric motors. All of these machines continued to use the wringer and rinse tub arrangements. Most were emptied by removing a stopper or turning a valve to let the water flow into a nearby drain, a series of buckets, or out into the yard.

The solar dryers we used (commonly called clotheslines) were very inexpensive, but often turned into real challenges on windy days when attaching a double sheet or on bitter cold days when the clothes froze. We carried them inside stiff as boards to thaw out. Other hazards, such as a clothesline breaking under the load of wet laundry, stray animals passing through the clothes, or children with dirty hands making an impromptu teepee of the wet sheets added to the 'joys' of wash days.

The only good thing was wash days happened only once a week. Until next Monday, we pushed the washer and rinse tubs back into the corner and went on with the duties of Tuesday, Wednesday, and the rest of the week.

Now I wash clothes with very little effort. It is so easy I do it almost every day. Actually, I never really get it done all at once.

I wonder, is this progress?

DISHWASHER AT THE ENDS OF MY ARMS

We have lived in two homes where we had a dishwasher. In our present home, the only dishwasher I have is at the end of my arms. During the holiday weekend when I was washing dishes inside while members of my family were outside getting ready for fireworks, I wished for an automatic dishwasher again.

I remembered my childhood when I stood in a hot kitchen washing dishes while others were outside playing in the cool evening breeze. (I realize that on other nights, I was the one outside playing while one of my sisters had the dishwashing chore. But somehow I mainly remember the times when I was the one inside.)

My mother never let the dishes go from one meal to another. With a family of eight children that is very understandable. There wouldn't have been enough dishes to serve the second meal without washing them first. I sometimes begged to let the dishes go for just a little while, but she was firm in wanting the dining room and kitchen cleaned and ready for the next meal before we did anything else.

Therefore, when we sat down to eat, we put a teakettle of water on the stove to heat for the dishwashing. If we had a jovial dinnertime, sometimes the water would reach the boiling stage before we were ready, but usually, since this was a very large tea kettle, the timing would be about right.

When we carried the dishes to the kitchen, cleared and stacked them in order, we put a small amount of the boiling water into the large dishpan before adding enough cold water to reach the temperature the dishwasher could tolerate. We put little pieces of dried cakes of soap into a small metal, mesh-like box on the end of a handle. We swished this box of soap pieces through the hot water until suds appeared. (I was a teenager before we could buy dishwashing soap chips, and then later, soap granules.)

In our home, we had a sink with a drain and cold water faucets. We also had a drainboard. Many homes at the time did not have a sink, drain, running water, or drainboard. The dishwasher used two large dishpans set on a table or stove top. One was for washing the dishes, the other for rinsing them. After rinsing, they always had to be hand dried. The rinse water was as hot as possible. We poured the boiling hot water over the dishes which we stacked on a rack on the drainboard. To keep from burning their fingers, those who used the second pan method had to gingerly fish out the rinsed dishes.

I grew up pronouncing the words of this process as "warshing" the dishes and then "wrenching" them. It took many years of teasing before I learned the correct way to say the words. I still hear some of my friends pronouncing the words as I used to. Perhaps it is a Midwest accent.

So while I was washing dishes this past weekend, I realized, even without a dishwasher, I had a
pretty easy job compared to the way we women used
to do chore. Notice I said *women*. The men of that generation didn't have a clue what went on in the kitchen.

Come to think of it, I do have more than the dishwasher at the ends of my arms. Husbands are handy
these days too!

Section Four

A TIME TO SPEAK

Communication
Equals
Revelation

GREAT CAESAR'S GHOST!

I was thinking recently about words that we don't hear very often anymore. I heard an emcee on a game show use the word "swell." I realized that in my teen years it was one of my favorite words to express approval. I rarely use it now except to describe a geographic or medical condition.

Even "A-OK" is going out of style. I remember when my older siblings said that things were "okey-dokey" and "hunky-dorey." Current teens say things are cool. Or maybe they don't any more. It has been a week since I talked directly to a teenager. I am probably out of date already.

It is funny to listen to some of us trying to sound 'cool.' We give ourselves away very quickly unless we are in constant contact with the younger generation. I think I am ahead of the game if I can even understand what they mean, much less be able to respond in kind.

Words used to express anger, irritation, or pain have certainly changed. As I was growing up, I never heard words that described bodily functions used as swear words or as adjectives. Now many movies and some television shows feel they can't let more than a few minutes pass without the 'F' or the 'S' word. In the remake of *The Little Rascals* movie, I was surprised to see that even though they had recreated the characters down to the hair styles and clothing, they put modern, slightly off-color words in their mouths.

I did a survey of the participants at The Neighbors Center to see what words their parents used when they were mad. Some could not remember any such words. Others remembered "Darn it" or "Darn it to heck." In my own case, I remember my mother saying "Sugar!" or "Aw, sugar!" when she dropped something or the cake didn't rise as she wished.

My father had two phrases, one of which grew longer as his anger increased. The first was "Sam Hill." He used this when things began to get out of control. He repeated that name several times when we skidded on a wet road in West Virginia and backed over the side of the mountain. Fortunately, a tree stopped us. I don't remember that Sam Hill came back into the conversation for a while.

When my father was angry he said, "Caesar." When he was even madder, he said, "Great Caesar." But when he was furious, he said, "Great Caesar's Ghost!" Then we knew it was time to disappear for awhile.

I am sure there were people in the neighborhoods where I grew up that used stronger words, but as a child I was not exposed to them. Even the books I read rarely used what I would call swear words. That is why Rhett Butler's "Frankly, my dear, I don't give a damn!" was so memorable to our generation. We were really living on the edge when we could repeat that phrase!

But shucks! Now I don't give a hoot, and it makes me no never mind if my language dates me. I couldn't care less. No sweat!

TEACHING IN NINETY-SECOND SEGMENTS

My great-granddaughter spent Friday night with me. On Saturday morning I turned on the television to get the usual Saturday morning cartoons that I remembered my children and grandchildren watching. Was I in for a surprise!

There was a science/learning-type program that I thought might be good, even though she was only four years old. I fondly remembered the Mr. Wizard shows my children watched and thought this would be like that. Not so! This one moved so fast that when Marilyn asked me what something was, it was gone. I couldn't follow what they were saying. Well, they weren't really saying it. They were yelling it while making all sorts of weird faces and getting into grotesque positions. The program was about invertebrates, using amoebas as an example.

One flash picture showed children acting out what it would be like to be an invertebrate. An excellent idea, but they flashed it on for maybe ninety seconds and then were on to something else. When Marilyn saw what they were doing and got interested, they had already changed to another presentation.

Some children may thrive on this type of learning, but our little one isn't geared that fast. She will sit for twenty minutes putting pegs into holes or fastening parts of plastic Easter eggs together.

I changed to another program more suited to her age and interest. I found cartoons where characters were 'zapping' one another with space-type weapons, cartoons of more weird-looking people putting children in scary predicaments, and one calmer story about children living in space.

After seeing this array of possibilities for children, I decided I am an old fogey. Are children really so speeded up these days that the ninety-second lesson is a good teaching tool? Where are the stories, as unrealistic as they were, about Lassie, Black Beauty, or Rin Tin Tin? Those stories followed an interesting plot and the good guys always won, even if the dogs and horses were wise beyond any animal possibilities.

Later we ate in a restaurant that had a coin video machine. We didn't supply any money, but the machine continually projected pictures showing explosions, lightning-like flashes again 'zapping' other objects, and lots of fast-paced action. Marilyn was fascinated, but, thankfully, hadn't learned yet that it got even more exciting if someone put money into the slots.

Later at home, we calmly read a story about the first Christmas. We sang, acted out the Itsy Bitsy Spider and his adventures with a water spout, and played with the lettered tiles of an adult game. I thought, this child is no different from her earliest ancestors enjoying the same pastimes as they did. So why do commercial interests insist that everything has to be so fast paced for children these days? Surely there are others who would also like to slow things down a bit.

I find some of the evening adult programs move too fast for me to really enjoy. The two or three concurrent plots switch back and forth so rapidly that sometimes I get mixed up on which of those good-looking men is the bad guy and which is the good guy. For that reason, I welcome the Hallmark specials, which usually are quiet one plot stories that let us understand and know the characters as the action progresses. A story that makes me cry has to be one that also immerses me in the narrative and the characters. I wonder if future generations raised in this speeded-up version of life will also enjoy a quiet drama in the evening.

I'm sure that the people who sat behind our family in church Sunday wonder what quiet, calm child I am talking about, because she squirmed, moved, and changed activities constantly. Maybe if the preacher presented his sermon in ninety-second sound bytes, she would have paid more attention, but he certainly would have lost all of us middle age plus members. We seem to be tortoises in the race of life. But remember who won in that fable.

WHAT'S CARBON PAPER?

I remember the thrill I had when I reached the third grade in Janney School in Washington, D.C. That was the year they let us put ink in the little ink well at the top right-hand corner of our desks. This also meant that our school supplies now included a pen with removable points that we stuck into the elongated holder. We used these points until they got too blunted to write well.

We must have come home with inky hands at the end of each day. I certainly remember some of the inky blotches on my papers. We kept a small blotter inside our desks to try to correct some of the over-abundance of ink we were bound to use.

About the time I reached junior high school, I owned a fountain pen. Though these pens were probably available earlier, I didn't have one to use. In our lockers we kept a small bottle of ink to refill the fountain pen when it went dry--usually at a very inappropriate time. I used a fountain pen as part of my daily equipment for years. I know a few people who still prefer to use them over the new thing--the ball point pen!

The invention of ball point pens has been a boon to all generations. Little children can use them without spilling ink. Older people with arthritic hands can get a brand that writes easily without much pressure. Campaigners and other advertisers use them for miniature billboards. They fit so nicely in shirt pockets that they often go through the wash in a white shirt pocket. I don't recommended this, however.

I use ball point pens for many writing needs, to solve my crossword puzzles, to jot down notes by the telephone, to sign my name when someone wants one of my books autographed, and of course, to write checks. But not for just plain writing.

Now my main communication tool is the computer with its capacity for e-mail. For years I resisted this trend, saying I was perfectly happy with my pen and paper. But once I got hooked, I got hooked. Now I feel a burden when I need to write someone who doesn't have e-mail. It really isn't too much of a chore since I can type and print it easily on the computer's word processor.

I just sent out identical letters to twenty members of a committee I chair. It was a very little problem. I typed the letter, ran the copies off on my machine, and could have printed labels for the envelopes if I had ever gotten around to entering this group into the computer.

As I was addressing the envelopes, I thought back to the first duplicating machine I experienced in sixth grade. It was a horrible purple duplicator. My teacher rolled a gummy sheet of some sort across a drum so that papers with purple words and numbers came off.

Later when I learned to type, I mastered carbon paper. After several times when my carbon ended up on the back of the original, I learned to face the shiny side away from me. Still later came the electronic typewriter. I thought there was no need to advance any farther because that machine could do wonders, especially if the office had a copy machine.

But now with my computer, I have everything in one set-up. I type my material and save it for posterity inside my computer before printing out a copy for me to keep. If it goes to the newspaper, I forward a copy to Jeffrey at the office by the e-mail attachment and don't even have to drive to town. What's more, my grandchildren, siblings, and anyone else who wants to, can access my writing on the Internet and read it on their own computer screen.

Since kindergarten children learn to use the computer in school right away, I wonder what they look forward to in third grade. After all, you can't put a girl's pigtail in a computer.

NECKSURGERY

I am very conscious of my neck this week because I had one of those lovely age spots taken off the front of my neck. While healing, the stitches made wearing certain dresses and blouses uncomfortable because they fit tightly around my neck. In searching through my wardrobe to find something that didn't irritate that spot (in front of what would be my Adam's apple if there wasn't so much flesh around it), I have given more thought to that part of me that holds my head up.

To complicate the problem, I also had a spot removed from the top of my spine where those cute little trademark labels made of coarse, firm materials made a sore. The biggest trouble with ordering clothing from a catalog is that I can't see what kind of torture device the designers have sewn in the back of the neck. Shopping in person allows me to inspect that aspect of the garment before I buy it. Cutting the label out doesn't completely relieve the problem because there is often a stiffness left in the seam where the material for the label has been sewn in. Also, if I do cut the label off I usually can't remember what laundry instructions were included on the tag.

But back to my neck. When I was skinny I used to think my neck looked a little like a goose's neck. Those days are gone forever. Now I am afraid it looks more like snow drift that has begun to melt slightly. Though turtle neck blouses have become one of my favorite styles, they can get rather warm in the summer.

Many of the summer clothes feature a scooped neckline, or what they call a jewelry neck line. I lean more toward the Mandarin style or even those similar to the old English Queens—those with a lot of pleated materials up around the neck.

This emphasis on my throat area has also started me thinking about the words associated with this part of the body.

We used to refer to a couple as 'necking.' I don't hear that term much anymore. I wonder if youth even know what the word means. It was used when that body part was as far as couples allowed themselves to go in pre-marital love making.

A close race was often described as being 'neck to neck.' Actually if it was either horses or humans, it really was the head that was out front. But 'head to head' has a different meaning, so we can't say that. In horse races announcers usually say something like winning by a nose, but that is not often the case in races between humans.

When we take a chance or try something daring we can be described as 'sticking our neck out.' Again, it is more accurately the head that we stick out, because it is a rare person whose neck protrudes beyond the head.

Articles of clothing such as neckties or neckerchiefs are aptly named as are pieces of jewelry such as necklaces or neck pins. Chokers that are necklaces worn tightly around the neck don't have the word neck in their name, and they are not in favor in my jewelry box because I don't want to draw attention to that part of my body anymore. Besides, they can get very uncomfortable, especially if they are hinged in a way that causes them to pinch sometimes.

I have often said that middle age plus is a time when we can become more casual about our clothing and not worry about style as much as we did when we were trying to impress others. But my remarks here point out that there is still much to consider when remembering all the body flaws we want to hide or at least disguise. Since comfort is high on our list, for the next few days I will be happier wearing sweat shirts or very soft turtle necks. But I'll have to be sure they don't have a tag at the back or I'll really be sticking my neck out again.

THE MAILBOX MYSTIQUE

There is a certain mystique about having the mailbox some distance from the house so that you have to take a walk to get the mail. As a child on the farm in the summer, it was often my job to walk the quarter mile up to the main road to the mailbox. As the driveway and the main road were hard-packed dirt at that time, I usually did this errand barefooted. If it were rainy, I also went barefooted to enjoy squishing the mud between my toes.

Cars and road conditions were not always reliable in those days, varying from day to day the hour the mailman came. I often sat in the shade of the Osage Orange hedge trees waiting for the mail. There was always some mail because we received the *Nevada Daily Mail* as well as morning and evening editions of the *Kansas City Star* and *Kansas City Times* through the mail. Also, unless my father was home on vacation, we got his daily letter to my mother.

I sat in the shade of the trees with my feet in the fine dust in the ditch and looked south for a cloud of dust on the road which would signal that a car was approaching. If it wasn't the mailman, then it would be one of our neighbors who usually stopped to say hello.

If my sister, Ellen, went with me to get the mail, we would play a game in the dusty road while waiting. After I became the owner of a bicycle, I often rode my bike to the mailbox and brought back the mail in the basket on the handlebars.

During the winter when we lived in Washington, D.C., our mail was dropped into a box by the front door twice a day, and our papers were thrown onto our porch both morning and night. I don't remember being very interested in what was in the mail in the winter. I was busy with school and neighborhood friends. The arrival of a dusty mail car was not a highlight of my day.

Now I live year-round near that same rural mailbox. Our own box is about a quarter of a mile away from our house. Since the public road and our driveway are both graveled now, walking barefooted to get the mail would be quite painful. The mail usually comes about the same time each day. We still get the local paper through the postal service, but our *Kansas City Star* is delivered at our road early each morning. The contents of the mailbox are not as interesting to me now, as they usually contain either bills we have to pay or advertisements of products we should buy to generate some more bills.

Since the advent of e-mail, I don't usually receive many personal letters, but the flood of get-well cards to Lester when he was ill brought back the thrill of going after the mail. Along with opportunities to get rich in yet another sweepstakes, there were notes and cards from friends both locally and away. These notes reminded me that the best modern communication device in the world can't equal the personal touch of a family member or old friend.

Perhaps the effort of going up to get the mail also makes the contents of the box more exciting.

The telephone answering machine and e-mail messages which can be sent or retrieved at any hour make it very possible and easy for us to be in touch with those we love. I wonder if it had been possible for my father to e-mail my mother each day as he traveled in his job to many states during the summer, whether the message would have meant as much to her as the letter written on some hotel stationery and mailed the next morning before he left for the day.

There is a mystique about what will be in the mailbox each day. I am quite sure that I, as a child, would not have been as aware of this daily contact with us if I had not hand-carried his letter the quarter mile from the mailbox to our home each day.

I need to hurry. I want to fax a note to my daughter before she leaves her office.

WAIT A MINUTE

I think I am a relatively patient person. I can wait while a child laboriously ties her shoes when I could do it in half the time. I can read a book without turning to the back pages to see how it comes out. Long movies are a treat, and waiting for food at a restaurant gives me time to enjoy people watching. But there are times when I am not at all patient. Some waits seem much too long.

When I was waiting for results of a medical test and a three day weekend slowed down the response from the lab, several weeks passed in what was really only a six day period of waiting for the answers. The wait seemed longer because we couldn't make any plans until we heard.

Our great-granddaughter frequently uses the phrase, "I can't wait until..." While in this limbo land of waiting, she is eager for her Uncle Kevin and Aunt Kelly to visit, for summer school to start, or for time to leave on a family trip to Virginia.

As a child, I remember the same impatience while looking forward to a special event. Although my mother used to tell me, "Don't wish your life away," I kept right on wishing for time to pass. Now in my middle age plus years I understand completely what my mother meant. I know that time doesn't take as long as it used to. Usually. But there are periods when it takes much longer.

Waiting for a loved one to arrive from a delayed plane trip can make minutes seem like hours. The concern about what caused the delay and the feeling of powerlessness add to the discomfort. Being put on HOLD on the telephone is another time when seconds turn into minutes. The nice music I hear while waiting can ease the pain a bit, but I really prefer to choose my own tunes. Waiting for a person to return my telephone call right away sometimes makes me wonder what right away really means. Often I need to use the phone again but need to keep the line open for the expected call which never seems to come.

Woodrow Wilson High School in Washington, D.C., had a two minute warning bell before the end of each class period. Those two minutes which I experienced seven times a day during my high school years seemed to never end. I liked school and enjoyed most of my classes, but this period of readiness made me restless to move on to the next thing. Now I realize it must have been even longer for the teachers!

Standing in line has never been a favorite pastime for me. At United Methodist Women events we are often treated to an evening banquet in a ballroom. The doors are scheduled to open at a certain time, but invariably over half of the women will arrive ten to fifteen minutes early. They stand around the doors wanting to be the first to enter and save seats for special friends. I sometimes think we look like refugees crowding forward to get a bite of food before the Care packages run out. That is, I think that until I take another look at our figures and decide that not many of us have missed many meals. You may be wondering how I know about the women crowding at the door to stand and wait. Well, you didn't think I was going to be the last one through the door, did you? If all the others didn't arrive early, there would be no reason for me to be standing there either!

I am reminded of a World War II song called, "Waiting for the Train To Come In." The words convey feelings of hope, concern, impatience, eagerness, or dread that are common experiences during waiting periods.

I started out by saying that I didn't mind the period of waiting between ordering food and receiving it in a restaurant. But I got to thinking about the name for people who serve us in these establishments. Do you think the title implies that the service will not be instant? Maybe that is why they are more often called servers today instead of waitresses or waiters.

NEEDLESS WORRIES

I had a heady experience lately. My American Association of University Women Book Club chose my book to discuss. And I was there! I was nervous at first, wondering how I would handle any criticisms or lack of enthusiasm. My sister says that a writer has to have a tough skin if there is to be any improvement. But if I had too tough a skin, I couldn't be sensitive to some of the things I like to write about.

I have attended writers groups where someone's unpublished work was critiqued for improvement before submitting it to a publisher. Some of the questions asked would have thrown me. One was, "What was your purpose in this paragraph?" Gosh, I don't know that I have a purpose in any of my paragraphs. I am just telling a story or talking about something. If I tried to analyze my purpose, I'm afraid I would never get anything written.

Maybe my purpose is to be spontaneous. Who knows? I just write what pops in my head. Sometimes I come back and decide that I'd better leave out something I wrote, but I sure don't have a pre-designed plan before I start.

I knew my local group couldn't ask me specific questions about my intentions. The genius moderator of our group gave definite guidelines for our discussions. We were to discuss the ideas within the content as it speaks to us. She asked each of us, at random, pertinent questions which the whole group could expound on after the initial answer.

Those instructions made me even more nervous. What can my foolishness say to this group of predominately younger women? Our discussions are planned to take between one and one and a half hours. After two hours our moderator had to call it quits though the conversation was still going strong. Believe it or not, the women found much to share in the five essays chosen for discussion. And they were kind to me, also.

My insecurity at this discussion reminded me of the many times when I have been apprehensive about a situation and found that I had made the wrong impression because of my self-centeredness.

One instance stands out in my mind from a Christmas season some thirty years ago. I was taking our youngest daughter to get special shoes at a store on the Plaza in Kansas City. The three older children were in school and Lester was in seminary in Kansas City. Our money was tight with his school expenses, but I had decided to make the day a special treat for Susan since she didn't like the shoes we had to have her wear for a couple of years for a weak ankle problem.

I took her to a tea room on the Plaza for lunch where we were seated at a small table next to an older woman at another table. (She was probably about the age I am now, but then, to me, she looked pretty old!) This woman had a fur stole and several large rings on her hands. Her clothes were straight out of a fashion magazine.

I suddenly was very aware of my run-down shoes and casual clothes. Our neighbor kept watching us throughout the meal as I became more and more aware of the differences between us. To compensate, I kept up a cheery conversation with Susan about what we would do next and the Christmas gifts we would buy for her siblings. As I invited responses from her, she chatted away merrily. All the while the woman kept watching the two of us. Determined not to let this spoil the occasion for Susan, I avoided looking her way.

Finally, she rose to leave. As she passed our table, she put her hand on my shoulder saying, "I hope you and your family have a very happy Christmas. You don't know how fortunate you are." Then to Susan, with tears in her eyes, she added as she left, "You are a precious child. Have a good time today."

I was stunned. I had been so preoccupied with the imagined criticism I felt in her presence that I mistook her interest in us entirely. Instantly I wanted to know more about this lady. Why the tears? What would her Christmas be like? Did she have family, or had she lost a child? Through the window I watched her walking toward one of the expensive apartment buildings nearby. I waved at her but couldn't tell if she saw me or not. I looked at Susan and thought about the others back home in school and realized that yes, indeed, I was the lucky one.

So it was with the members of the book club. I shouldn't have been apprehensive. I am blessed to have friends who can enjoy discussing the merits of purses, bosses, and even the force of gravity, the topics of the chosen essays.

If all my worries turn out so well, I am wondering what I can find to worry about. Maybe improper sentence structure?

BUMPER STICKERS

Have you read any good bumper stickers lately? This phenomenon is relatively new, that is, we middle age plus drivers did not have such things on our cars, if we had cars, when we were young. Maybe we would see a school or college sticker occasionally.

It is not only the young who have these messages on their cars. Many retirees have such slogans as, "I'm spending my kids' inheritance" or descriptive phrases such as "I'd rather be fishing (or golfing)."

What amazes me is that people of all ages are willing to drive all over town with bumper stickers of questionable taste plastered all over their cars. Some have their bumpers filled up and attach the sticker wherever they can find a spot. I followed a car that had four slogans on the back. One stated, "My son can beat up your honor student." Another proclaimed the driver to be the equivalent of a female dog, but stated that she was d— good at it. The third asked us not to tailgate, but those were not the words used. Actually the slogan got rather specific about a physical condition that could affect the back part of a person's anatomy and requested that if we were not in that condition to stay off the back of that driver. (This translation loses some of the vulgarity, but I did not want to repeat what I considered poor taste.) The fourth bumper sticker referred to another bodily function that happens but is not usually proclaimed on our cars.

I wondered what burly-looking, tough woman would drive a car with all of these vulgar sayings stuck on the back. I speeded up a bit to catch sight of the driver and saw a very nice-looking woman, probably in her forties, driving carefully down Austin Street. As she saw me looking at her, she flashed a very warm smile at me and gave a half wave. I couldn't help wondering if she was driving someone else's car or if to her these slogans were not offensive.

The one that bothered me the most was the one about her kid beating up my honor roll student. If she really had a child, what message is that giving to the young student? I'll admit that academic achievement isn't the only talent to brag about concerning your child, but being able to beat up someone is certainly not something I would choose to flaunt.

I've seen equally questionable slogans on RVs of older people and also across the front of ball-type caps. Some words that were considered in poor taste a few years ago are now used freely in all sorts of gatherings. Therefore, putting them in black and white (or red, purple or green) on your car or on your clothing is probably the next logical step. I couldn't do this, but I guess each person's taste is an individual choice.

Several years ago there was a series of bumper stickers with a similar theme. "Bikers do it in the dirt," "Farmers do it in the field," "Teachers do it with class," were some of the samples. When following a teacher's car with that slogan, I mentioned to my preacher-husband that he ought to devise one for ministers. He immediately came up with, "Preachers do it for eternity!" Our son had a tee-shirt made for him with that slogan. It pleased Lester very much, but he doesn't wear it in public, nor would he put it on the car as a bumper sticker.

However, maybe one could be fashioned that says, "Honk if you are middle age plus!"

NUMBERS ADD UP

I have resisted memorizing certain numbers that identify me. If I am asked for my Social Security number, I have to get out my billfold to see my card. Not knowing such a vital number may appear to be stupid, but for me it is a protest of sorts. We are all known by so many numbers that I feel it is foolish to clutter up my memory bank with a bunch of numbers. I would much rather fill my mind with names. But I am finding remembering names gets harder and harder.

Think about all the numbers that identify each of us. First is our birth date. That one I can remember. Then there is our address, which includes a five and/or nine digit zip code in addition to house number, or route, and box number. Next is our telephone number. Remember when we used to simply ask for the person we were calling. Later, the exchanges were names such as Columbia (dialed as C-O-L) followed by four numbers? Now we have to add the area code for long distance. In our case, when we want to dial our nearest neighbors to the south, we have to punch 1 for another exchange, then the 417 area code, and finally seven more numbers. It's easier to hop in the car and go see them!

We have telephone calling card numbers with a secret pin number that only those of us using the card know. If we want to use the handy ATM machine at a bank, we have to remember another secret number to punch in after we use all the numbers on our card. Though these protections are for our benefit, I find it difficult to remember which pin number goes with which longer number.

Now that our driver's license number is the same as our Social Security number, that eliminates one number. But we still have all the numbers on our checking account, our credit cards, and different account numbers from orders we have placed or services we receive.

Many who are middle age plus have an e-mail number and a fax number. We have to get used to adding a dot or dash in between numbers or letters when we are writing friends with our new technologies.

All these numbers add up to my firm conviction that I'd rather try to remember your name than to know that I've got your number. I will carry an address book to record all the necessary numbers for my family and friends, but I have all I can do to come up with your name.

YOU KNOW

You know, I've been thinking about, you know, writing about the way, you know, that some people talk these days. Have you noticed how often young adults and teenagers throw in the unneeded phrase, "You know."

We were listening to a local television station interview with several college-age football players. These good looking, smart young men put the phrase, "You know," in almost every sentence. I guess it is a replacement for the "uhs" and "ers" we sometimes use to fill the silence while our brain tries to keep up with what we are saying.

Other people use more offensive words as punctuation in their sentences. Some cannot carry on a conversation without a bodily function word in almost every sentence. I prefer "You know" to that.

Back in the dark ages, when my generation was young, we also had our own conversation fillers. I overused the word "swell." When I needed an adjective to describe something good, I used "swell" rather than trying to come up with an alternative. My sister-in-law, Jean, who was an English teacher when I was in junior high, looked at one of my assignments before I turned it in. She suggested I not use "swell" so much. I probably argued with her that it was a very good word, but I tried to reduce my usage of that word from that time.

Jean's suggestion represents one of the pluses of having a big family. I not only have the 'guidance' (sometimes called bossiness) of all my siblings, I can also learn from their spouses. My brother-in-law, Alex, a skilled linguist, introduced me to all sorts of new words that were fun to use, but my mother did not want me to use some of them. His delightful sense of humor sometimes became a bit earthy. However, he never used the common bodily function words that are so prevalent now. His conversation was much more subtle with double meanings making the phrases hilarious.

I learned some great phrases from the South from Lida, my oldest brother's wife, and historical phrases from our Civil War buff, Dudley, the first in-law to enter the family.

Since Vernon's Dorothy and Ellen's Lane were nearer my own age, we shared many of the same experiences except that Lane was well versed in hunting and fishing lore of the Ozarks and Dorothy was a big city girl from Rochester, New York. I'm sure I also picked up words and information from each of them.

Then the weekly radio shows that we always listened to added to our vocabulary. A regular greeting was Jack Benny's "Jello, again." I still find myself answering, "Is somebody bawling for Beulah?" when I am asked to do some household chore for another person. I'm sorry to say I imitated some of the phrases on Amos and Andy, especially those used by the Kingfisher. Our family quite often used the phrase from

World War II, "Is this trip really necessary?" especially when someone was monopolizing the bathroom.

We used to be able to tell where people came from by their accents and words they used. Now with most families watching the same television shows and movies, we have blended our patterns of speech and include words and meanings unknown to us in our childhood.

But each generation, you know, seems to come up with, you know, their own, you know, style. And thankfully most of these trends do pass. That's really swell!

WHAT'S THAT, YOU SAY?

Our English language is hard to understand at times. Words can have opposite meanings, or words that are spelled differently are pronounced the same. All of this makes it a difficult language. But something else has been bothering me lately, namely the use of phrases to make a point, when the phrases don't seem to make much sense.

Yesterday I heard a news interview where the interviewer accused his guest of pushing the envelope. Now I know that it means he was going a little beyond what is acceptable or safe. But what on earth does an envelope have to do with safety? I push envelopes across my desk each day and don't have any feeling that I am doing a risky thing. I have received some paper cuts from envelopes at times, but that is as far as any danger has occurred. So where does the saying come from and what does it mean, literally?

It puts me in a *Catch 22* situation. I can use the phrase for its accepted meaning but feel uncomfortable because I don't really understand the meaning. And just where did this *Catch 22* phrase come from? Why is it 22, and not 21 or 23? I know the phrase means we are in a dilemma but why the numbers?

Some sayings are more understandable. When I am ready to hit the hay, catch some Z's, or take a snooze I understand that sometimes people did sleep on mattresses stuffed with hay or maybe took a quick nap in a haystack when no one was looking. Catching some Z's, of course, refers to the sound a person makes when sleeping. The 'Z' letter has been used in comic strips for years to tell us that the character is asleep. Snoozing perhaps includes snoring and dozing into one word but I am not sure of that.

Along that same line, we can understand fairly well, to take five, take a breather, or get a little shut-eye. We have many sayings about resting and sleeping.

We have even more phrases about eating. Such as I'm ready to put on the feed bag, chow down, catch a bite, feed my face, or raid the refrigerator. Most people know what they mean, except those new to the language. Putting on a feed bag makes no sense when the listener has no knowledge of how work horses were fed. Chow down might be confused with a breed of dog, catching a bite could seem to be talking about going fishing, and raiding the refrigerator might sound war-like.

Advertising slogans take on a life of their own and are easily understood, unless the hearer has not watched any of our television broadcasts. "Please, Mother, I'd rather do it myself," "Where's the beef?" and "I can't believe I ate the whole thing" were common sayings in the 1970s and 80s. Though not used as much as in the past, most people still understand their meaning. Newer slogans urge us to "Just do it, "Just say no," or to dial a certain number. Not many of us have dials on our phones now. Somehow it doesn't sound right to say, "Punch 10-10-whatever."

Also consider the sports page. Taken literally the headlines make no sense. "Red Sox Trample Eagles" sounds rather impossible even if sox could actually walk. "Tigers Trounce Panthers" would make us scurry for shelter in the wilderness of wild animals. When the "Royals beat the Cardinals," it sounds like cruelty to small animals.

I have probably pushed the envelope of your patience far enough by now with all this talk about our language. Since I majored in English in college, I find it very interesting, but I know some of my readers will say enough already. So I won't belabor this subject anymore. And that's my final answer.

Section Five

A TIME TO LOVE

A circle of love
Has no beginning or ending.

IT SEEMS TO ME I'VE HEARD THAT SONG BEFORE

I have just spent two and a half hours listening to songs from the 1940s. Two compact discs contain enough memories to keep me going for many days. In all forty-two of these songs, the one aspect I couldn't miss was ROMANCE. I noticed it not just because they were the songs we sang and danced to during our dating years but it is because the songs themselves are romantic.

None dealt with untrue lovers. The theme of being left behind was due only to wartime orders and responsibilities.

Admittedly, the 1940s was a romantic time because of the war and loneliness both for the service men and those at home. But I couldn't help thinking as I listened to these songs again that maybe a good dose of romance would be helpful now. Today many songs, movies, and television shows have more to do with passion than with romance. A situation that led to the hope of holding hands in the 1940s, now is portrayed as a chance to jump into bed. Many of the songs speak of dreaming of a chance to be together or of sustaining love and memories.

Even the music is romantic. It invites a dreamy, quiet close-together dance or a walk in the moonlight holding hands. The very titles reflect the mood. "Now Is the Hour," "Always," "A Sleepy Lagoon," "Moonlight Becomes You," and "You'd Be So Nice to Come Home to" all portray a type of romantic love we don't see or hear in today's media.

If I am playing this music when my grown kids (baby boomers) come home, they usually make some remark about "Mom's music again." They prefer the songs of the 1960s and 70s. That is fine, but I will wait to see which ones live longer.

In the book of 'golden oldies,' we find more songs that are romantic than any other kind. There must be something in us that yearns for romance, even if we do not always find it in real life.

When we are middle age plus, we remember and have enjoyed many changes in music and entertainment. It's not surprising that many of my special memories are tied up with Bing Crosby, Guy Lombardo, and Dinah Shore. But then, one of the songs on the disc is "To Each His Own."

A PART OF HISTORY

Since March is Women in History Month, I started thinking about my former neighbor women. These women will never be in any history book but they certainly are worthy of more than a mention in the history of our neighborhood.

Starting a mile west of our home, I fondly remember Faye Halcomb. She was the flower lady to me. Whenever she came to our home, whether it was for a neighborhood gathering or just to visit my mother, she brought a large bouquet of flowers. Gladioli were her specialty, but I also remember zinnias and other colorful gifts. This touch of beauty in her garden along with the vegetables made a bright spot as we drove past her house. Sharing this beauty was a touch of class that I will always remember.

Moving around the corner toward the east, we come to Mrs. Watson's home. The house itself wasn't anything special, but inside was an elegance that was distinctive of this lady. She had pieces of crystal, china, and other pretty things that we didn't display in our home because of so many children. Mrs. Watson was the 4-H leader who taught us girls about manners, table settings, and other social niceties. But more importantly, she was one of the pillars of the community Sunday School, serving as superintendent for years. Many town churches would have been pleased to have the attendance rate that this little non-denominational group maintained.

Across the road was Mrs. Eaton. Her children were close family friends of my siblings which made her even more special. I loved to sit and talk with her. She treated me as her guest, listened to my conversation, and added her comments as if I were a grown woman visiting her. I loved to walk through the pasture from our house to hers, and I also loved to smell the aroma of jelly and homemade bread that often came from her kitchen.

Then there was Mrs. Horn. She was more like a surrogate grandmother to all of us Gray children. She knew when we left our house and when we returned. She watched for our greeting cards when we were in Washington and commented if any were missing. ("Vernon's must have gotten lost in the mail," she'd say.) But this woman who survived abandonment from her first husband, death of two of her children in adulthood, loss by fire of the nice home she shared with her second husband, and finally widowhood and poor health in her last years, never lost her concern and love for her neighbors and her family.

Then across our road, I remember Mrs. Maple with her sparkling brown eyes and sense of humor. She worked many long and hard hours with her family, the garden, and house, but she always had time for a few minutes of fun with the kids who would gather in her home.

And of course, in my eyes, my own mother is an excellent example of the gifts that generations of unsung heroines gave to our country. But she is a complete topic of her own.

These women were a part of history even though they do not appear by name in our textbooks. But without the beauty, graciousness, sharing of ideas, concern, and fun that my neighbors showed the young ones in the area, this community could not have produced so many solid citizens who still contribute to our world.

Though we probably will not be recorded in history either, I hope that we can do half as good a job of contributing to the next generation as these women. They really are in history as they live on in our memories and in the values they shaped in us.

A VISION IN FLANNEL

Last week two incidents happened within a few hours that were closely related and yet opposite in nature. Since I haven't been able to stop thinking about them, I am sharing my thoughts with you.

I was getting my hair cut in the beauty shop and noticed the addition to the shop that cleverly is called "Undercover Creations." I walked through the racks of shimmering undies, negligees, and gowns, admiring the styles and materials, all the while thinking, "I'm glad another shop has opened in town for fine things, but these are not for me." I expressed this out loud and was shown a section that could be for me. The garments were more modest and could also cover an ample figure. Robes and full length nightgowns (I'm a pajama person myself!) were attractively displayed. Since I received some flannel nightwear for Christmas, I was not tempted to buy but was again pleased that we have one more place in town where we may make choices.

I left with these visions of silk and satin dancing in my head as I drove to return a book we had borrowed from a neighbor. It was still fairly early in the morning, and I hadn't thought about it perhaps being too early for a retired couple to be up. When I arrived at the farm home, a friendly dog greeted me and a not-so-friendly-sounding dog barked at me from an enclosed pen. Other times I had been at the home someone would appear at the door as soon as I drove up, but today no one came until I rang the bell.

The door was opened a bit and then when the lady of the house recognized me, it was opened a bit further. This lovely lady stood sheepishly grinning in a floor-length flannel nightgown with lace around her pretty face. I handed her the book and apologized for not having called first. Then my friend told me that this was her eighty-seventh birthday. She was celebrating by being lazy.

The smile on her face framed by the lacy neckline made as pretty a picture as you could find anywhere. With simplicity she radiated the qualities that each of us hope for in our older years.

I didn't stay but a minute but the vision of this moment has stayed with me ever since. Norman Rockwell couldn't have painted a better picture of everyone's ideal grandmother waiting at the door.

I was amused at her embarrassment at being caught still in her nightclothes in mid-morning. Her generation has equated early rising with being proper. But her pleasure in giving herself this birthday celebration of being lazy warmed my heart. She not only had the conviction to do it, but she was obviously taking pleasure in it.

Hearing a motor behind the barn, I assumed her husband was outside doing some task. I hoped he had prepared his own breakfast and let her sleep in. Knowing him, I imagine he would have done just that.

Then I thought back to the beautiful garments I had seen on the racks earlier that day. The prettiest model in the world wouldn't have looked any better in those nice creations than my friend did in her flannel gown. I tried to envision what she (or I) would really look like in the new apparel in town and decided that neither of us would benefit from most of the styles. Actually it wasn't the lace-trimmed gown that made such a pretty picture in the farmhouse doorway. It was the smile on my friend's face that was so eye-catching.

And it is a lot cheaper.

SOME THINGS DO IMPROVE WITH AGE

I had a really good day yesterday. I had to stop at the grocery store on my way home from a meeting. For once I wasn't in a hurry. I took time to walk leisurely up and down each aisle checking on items I may have forgotten to put on my list. Sure enough, I remembered that I almost emptied my baking powder can the last time I used it. Then I saw some other items I don't usually notice when I am shopping in a hurry. I bought a few extras. I think that is called impulse buying, but heck, I may need that special type of dust rag when I get the house cleaned for the AAUW group that is coming next month.

One drawback to the day was that the store personnel had rearranged the dairy case so I almost bought the wrong brand of milk because my brand wasn't where it should have been. I think they wanted me to try this new brand they moved into the best spot. My son taught me a long time ago if it isn't broken, don't try to fix it. I liked the milk I had been buying, and it was cheaper too, so why change? The old brand was fine.

My favorite checker's line was the shortest. I would have chosen it even if it had been longer because I enjoy going through her line. A little older than some of the checkers, she is also friendlier and does the kind of job I like. She calls me by name, which is an ego trip for anyone, and she remembers what type of sacks I prefer.

After paying for my groceries (a little higher because of my leisurely shopping purchases) the carry-out lady said, "I will take these to your car for you." She didn't ask it as a question, which makes me feel that I am a lazy person to have someone push the cart into the lot and load my car. No, she said it as a fact. I thanked her the same way. She also is a bit older than some of the people who carry out groceries, but she is friendlier and more careful. When she finished, she wished me a good day and closed the door. Noticing that it didn't quite shut tight, she opened and reshut the door again. I appreciated that.

When I arrived home, I found that the mailman (ours is a man) had brought a package up to the house instead of leaving the annoying little note that said I could go back to town and pick it up at the post office. In addition, in the mail was an order for one of my books and a letter from a long-time friend who moved away. She writes nice notes and keeps in touch with her home town even though she is now living with her daughter. Opal Gould is older than some of my friends, but she certainly is friendly and one I love to hear from.

After I put away the groceries, I checked my e-mail. Another friend had sent me a cute picture of a wrinkled dog in a lawn chair with the saying that wrinkles are a sign of character.

Before starting on my work, I took a minute to sit down and read the paper while listening to a favorite CD of old songs of the 1940s. I could hear each word sung (of course I already knew most of them), and the tunes stayed in my head long after the CD finished playing. There were no deaths in the paper of any of my acquaintances, and I had a laugh at "For Better or Worse" in the funnies because the mother was going through a series of tests because of her age.

All in all, it was really a good day. I sense a pattern here somewhere. My day was made better in various ways by people who were friendly, considerate, and helpful without being asked. If I had been an old woman I would have really appreciated all the attention. Even being only middle age plus it made me feel good. My day showed that many things do improve with age—from check-out clerks in a store to music on a CD!

DIVERSITY GIVES STRENGTH

One of my grandfather's favorite stories was about a boy who went to the big city for one day. Having never been off the farm before, his experiences so excited him that he felt like a different person from the boy who left that morning. He swaggered up to his little sister as he returned and noticed the family cat. He said, "I see you still have the same old cat!"

My weekend was something like that. It was filled with many experiences, meeting old and new friends and having my eyes opened yet a bit more. When I came home after being gone only three days, I was almost surprised to see the same old cats.

The experience that made the biggest impact on me was riding and rooming with a woman who had been a victim of polio in her youth. She is now middle age, or maybe almost middle age plus, but she has lived for over fifty years with this disabling condition. Although she can walk limited distances with arm crutches, she uses a motorized wheel chair. Her van is equipped to lift her chair into the back and has hand controls for driving.

We have been friends for a long time, but this was the first time I spent much time with her and was privileged to be her support system. Twenty-five years of social work taught me much about those living with a disabling condition, but learning about a subject and living with it, even second hand, are two different things.

What I learned first is that when you are told that a place is wheel chair accessible, that doesn't mean it is easily accessible. Doors that opened toward my friend were a big road block since the front of her wheelchair/scooter protruded farther than her arm reach. Even if she could reach the door and open it toward her, it often would close before she could position herself inside the door to keep it open.

The bathroom in our supposedly accessible room had a tub with high sides. She could have managed a shower or a low tub, but she had to take sponge baths while seated on the closed stool.

Most people we met were very helpful to let us go first or to hold doors open. However, in one restroom on the way home there was a long line of women waiting. Though it was obvious that she was having some trouble standing on the slick floor, a very healthy-looking woman popped into the stall for disabled persons and didn't even apologize when she came out and couldn't help seeing the person such stalls are designed for.

But through all of these experiences it was I who got upset or mad, and not my friend. It's sad, but I think she was so used to these obstacles that she didn't worry about them and just looked to see what she would do in the situation. Her sense of humor and quiet appreciation of the event we were attending were blessings to everyone present.

The other experience that highlighted my weekend was a presentation by the Native Americans in our denomination's Oklahoma Missionary Conference about the history of the various tribes that are now part of Oklahoma. They depicted the Trail of Tears, mission schools, and church leaders, while singing hymns in the native tongues of each tribe. I know and have worked with many of these people on committees and during events, but seeing their long sad history portrayed with a hopeful ending, gave me added appreciation for my friends.

The entire event ended with the Native American women giving each of the 1,097 participants a seed bag containing three seeds, squash, corn, and bean. We were to plant them in one mound together so that the corn can give strength to the bean vine, the squash vine can retain the moisture around the roots of the corn, and the bean and corn provide shade for the squash. Thus the support each gives the others, in return, adds to the total life of each. Such support was evident for and from my friend in the wheelchair.

And we did still have the same old cats even though I had been away three long days!

THANKS TO MY SIBLINGS

I am blessed to have been born into a large family with multiple brothers and sisters. Sometimes people talk about a large family with disdain, as if we would all be dirty and ignorant. Large families are not too practical now with the high costs of living and educating children, but back when my siblings and I were raised, large families helped with the work load on farms or in family businesses.

When I was growing up, each sibling added something to my education, manners, and interests. Gertrude, who became a librarian, introduced me to good reading and also took Ellen, my next youngest sister, and me to many cultural events. Kathryn, who was the first to marry, was a good role model for me of what a wife and mother should be. Of course, I already had a wonderful role model in my own mother, but Kathryn brought it a step closer in age for me. Miriam, the eternal teacher, never stopped educating the rest of the family through her many travels, the schools she attended, and her life experiences. Each of my three brothers added to my understanding of sports, mathematics, writing, and social graces. All of these siblings together added to a very happy childhood filled with fun. I have left out one sister, because Ellen, sharing the younger role in this family with me, was my constant companion and leader. We shared everything from a double bed, to friends, and entertainment.

But what I am thinking about today is how much my brothers and sisters mean to me now. When we read in the paper about surviving family members of a person who has died, the brothers and sisters are listed, but we often fail to realize what a loss that death is to them. Usually they are no longer in the same household and the daily routine is not altered greatly by the death. But the loss of someone who has been a part of your life forever (especially if you are the baby of the family) is very great.

Your siblings are made of the same stuff as you are and in many cases have had the same or similar life experiences.

Each of the eight children in our family could paint a different picture of each of our parents, depending on age, the order of birth into the family, and the geographic and economic condition of the family during important years. But all of us have been part of the total relationship with both parent and with each of our siblings. We all knew the best friends of each other. We had common experiences even if they came in different calendar years.

We all knew we had to be home at six o'clock to eat supper with the family. The only deviation was if we weren't there, and then our mother left a plate in the oven for us. We knew not to interrupt our father when he was talking. We knew that we would have our turn at washing or drying the dishes unless we were a brother. Then other chores awaited.

We knew we were welcome to have friends in our home and nothing would embarrass us in front of our friends when they were there.

Shared memories, shared expectations, shared griefs, and shared joys form a strong nurturing foundation which doesn't diminish as we go separate ways in our adult lives. Each gap through death is painful, and yet the strength of the total family helps us share these experiences together.

I have seen coffee mugs with the slogan "Sisters Are Forever." I agree, and the same is true for brothers. I would never have changed our large family for a smaller one, and now as the number of original siblings is decreasing, we are blessed with nieces and nephews who help fill the gap and keep the old memories alive while adding new experiences for the family lore.

Sometimes when I am preparing a family dinner for twenty or so people I wonder what it would be like to have been an only child. After having experienced life with seven siblings, I doubt I could have been as happy as an only child. I am sure there are some only children out there who can't imagine life as we lived it in a house with no privacy, one bath room (or none) and lots of noise and activity. But I give thanks for it.

MY HISTORY TEACHER

I missed watching a little of the inauguration events on television Saturday because of a meeting. A friend who was also attending the meeting mentioned to me that she regretted missing the ceremonies. We visited with each other about opportunities we had in the past had to be physically present at historic events. Neither of us were really impressed at the time but have each come to realize that we have been privileged.

In Chris's case, her uncle took her to Adlai Stevenson's funeral and other special events while she was visiting him in Washington. In my case, my brother, Harold, gave me many opportunities to see history in the making.

I was not always interested at the time, but I have never turned down the chance to go anywhere with my big brother. So when he suggested I go with him and others in the family, I was always more than ready.

Because of his interest in being on the scene when history was being made, I was able to see the King and Queen of England when they came to visit President Franklin Roosevelt. They went by in an open car with FDR and Eleanor right down Pennsylvania Avenue. I couldn't help but notice the difference in Saturday's parade where the new President and his wife were in an enclosed limo with secret service personnel all around them. They did get out and walk a little and the weather was terrible, but times have changed so much that the days of seeing our Presidents in a convertible have passed.

Harold also took me to the White House lawn when Winston Churchill was visiting Roosevelt. We saw him light the national Christmas tree and heard him make a short speech.

Although I was here in Missouri at the time and didn't share this experience, Harold walked through the riot area of Washington in the 1960s to see what had happened. He didn't want to miss that nastier historic event either.

Today, in his nineties, he is very active in a movement by an organization of which he is past president, The Oldest Inhabitants of the District of Columbia. These are people who have lived in Washington, D.C. for many years. They are requesting that Pennsylvania Avenue be opened up again so that traffic can flow past the White House as it did in the past. Security measures caused the concern that closed off a portion of the famous avenue. Many organizations feel that it was not necessary to keep the public from the routes that were designed to insure a good flow of traffic past the historic places in the city.

While our family was traveling back and forth from Washington to Missouri each year during my childhood, Harold always wanted us to take the routes that would let us see the capitol buildings in each state that we crossed. Most of the family was more intent on getting the trip over with quickly and didn't care about looking at another building. But now I am grateful that I can envision so many capitol buildings and know that I actually drove past these structures.

Many people travel by air today and miss getting the feel of our great country that we experience when we drive. Even the present day interstate highways keep us from really becoming part of the country we travel through. In the past when the highways went down every main street of every town, travel was slow and tempers might have flared a bit. But we knew how towns in West Virginia differed from those in Kansas or Missouri. Eating in Mom and Pop restaurants also gave us the feel of each town. The franchise restaurants we use today are so similar we can't even remember where we ate from one day to the next.

Thanks to my big brother's interest in history, I feel a kinship to those who have made our nation great, whether it be a President or a main street business family in small town, USA.

Instead of being in the stands to view this year's inauguration, Harold stayed home and watched it on television. But his heart was downtown with the crowds.

A GERIATRIC VACATION

We just returned from a 3,000 mile, thirty-relative, car trip to the eastern coast. The route we traveled was very similar to the routes my family used to take twice yearly as we returned to spend the summers in Missouri from Washington, D.C. Although the states covered were the same, that ended the similarity.

The earliest family trips took four days with eight or nine of us in one car. One vivid memory is of Mama trying to comb all the snarls out of my hair before we went into a restaurant to eat after hours of having the wind blowing from the four lowered windows. Sometimes she just gave up and smoothed the top part down.

U.S. Highway 40, the route we took most often, went right down the main street of every town and to the very top of each mountain that we crossed. The family usually got out at the top of the mountain, relieved that the car had made it, and took a moment to see the view.

Our recent trip on Interstates didn't let us see most of the towns except as names on road signs. The incline in the mountains had been cut through the hills or tunneled under a peak until we hardly realized we were crossing the Alleghenies. The view from the highways was universal—dense trees on both sides of the roads with an occasional peek through to a small village below or the stacks of a factory in a nearby town. The trip took us only one and one half days including stops for meals and other necessities.

There were many changes also in the possibilities to take care of these necessities. When my family was traveling in the 1930s and 40s, every filling station had a one-holer woman's restroom which we entered from the outside of the station. The men's room was usually entered from within the station. But each station also had a nice drinking fountain, a man who came to wipe off our windshield, fill the radiator with water, and check our oil and tires.

On our recent trip, the only water we could get to drink had to be bought in little bottles along with soft drinks, tea, and juices. The pumps were so automatic that several didn't even allow us to go inside to pay but took our credit card in a slot from the outside. The only windshield cleaning was done by Lester, usually while I pumped the gas. The restrooms were often unisex ones inside a convenience store. At the big truck stops, the huge restrooms were so automatic that the toilet flushed as soon as you stood up and the water started when we put our hands under the faucet.

The biggest change, however, was the amount and speed of the traffic. We were in several traffic jams that lasted nearly an hour on four lane roads. When there was not a traffic jam, the cars and trucks moved so fast that when we set the cruise control on the speed limit, every other vehicle on the road passed us.

The worst traffic was from Washington up to Connecticut where we were going to celebrate a sister's ninetieth birthday. We had a pleasant time there with another sister we picked up in Washington and a few younger relatives, but we were very glad to get back to Washington to slightly slower and less dense traffic. The three Missourians of us (my sister from Lebanon joined us for the trip) were very glad to finally get west of Washington and out of the urban sprawl that the East has become.

The neighborhood where we were raised in Washington, spending hours on bikes, skates, and hiking in woods, is now covered with miles and miles of homes. The street we used to play in cannot be crossed without waiting for a lull in the traffic. It's really surprising what a mere fifty-five years can do to a growing city!

With all of this traffic, we experienced only one instance of road rage (that we knew of) when we paused at a turn to decide which way to go. The man behind us let us know that he would like to tell us where to go.

We visited our brother who was recuperating in Washington from a set-back. We celebrated with our sisters and saw various nieces and nephews. Lester spent some time in the National Archives finding information about his family, and we came home safely and in good time.

So, all in all, it was good experience. But we may not want to repeat it for another ninety years or so.

HOUSES AND
NEIGHBORHOODS CHANGE

Even though I have been home from our Eastern visit for over a week, I still keep mulling over the events and impressions of the trip. I have been back to the Washington area at least every two years since I left in 1943 to attend the University of Missouri. I have also been in the greater New York area more than once each decade since that time. However, on this trip I have gone back in my memory bank more deeply and noticed the changes more clearly than in earlier trips.

This phenomenon of being middle age plus makes the memories of the past more important and more cherished while creating an urge to share these remembrances. That is partly what makes younger people avoid conversational times with us. But they will reach the point where they will wish they had asked us more.

Visiting with our sisters and brother, we constantly were saying, "Miriam would have known," or, "I wonder what Mama thought when..." At the time we were too involved in our own busy lives to stop and wonder. Now we want to know.

I guess that is partly why I like to write these essays. It gives me a chance to be heard, and even if no one reads them, at least I have put my thoughts down on paper. Maybe when our children reach the stage where we are now, they can get some of their answers from a musty newspaper or a dusty book (if they haven't already thrown them all away!).

When I was a child and lived in Washington, D.C. during the school year, Western Avenue by our house was only three blocks long. There was much open space and just four large homes in this wonderful neighborhood. Now there are hundreds of houses, apartments, condominiums, and shopping centers. The change that bothered me the most was the outside of our old home. This three story house with a full basement was a wonderful place for our large family to grow up. Two sisters got married there, and we celebrated many special events inside those walls. The best part of the house was a large front porch which spanned the entire front of the house. A bay window in the living room made the porch partially divided into two sections with a narrower portion remaining which connected the two areas. A glider swing and other chairs supplemented the wide banister railing top which usually seated one or two children when the family sat outside.

The open part around the front door was the scene of many games including double dare as we challenged each other to jump off the top of the eight steps that led up to the porch. I remember the pride I felt when I finally was first brave enough to make the big leap. The wide sidewalk to the street was usually marked with hop scotch patterns or was the place for a snappy game of double Dutch jump rope or kids learning to roller skate.

The porch is now completely gone from the house. Although the bay window is still there, the house is shorn of its character. The traffic moves so swiftly now that I couldn't see if there are still eight steps to the front door, but I would think there would have to be.

I am cheered when I see some newer homes are again built with front porches. The whole feeling of neighborliness is enhanced when a front porch with comfortable chairs proclaims that the residents enjoy a friendly chat or will take the time to wave as a friend passes by.

That house is probably worth five times its value from when we lived there, but for me it has lost value along with its character. I would love to be like the brazen people on the hot-dog commercials and knock on the front door to tell the present owners that I used to live there. I wonder if they would invite me in, and if they did what changes I would find inside.

I'll bet the secret passageway underneath the attic steps has been sealed off (actually it was a loose slat in the stairs that could be removed and a skinny child could squeeze through the opening.)

Probably the owners wouldn't want to hear my memories of the home anymore than you poor readers do.

GOODBYES ARE HARD

When you are the youngest in a big family, you must learn to say goodbye to beloved relatives. But it never gets easy. One of these losses was my brother-in-law, Alex Toth, who died in suburban Washington, D.C.

When Alex's memorial service was held, I couldn't be there with my sister Gertrude and the family. I felt closer by sharing my memories with you.

Alex came from an Hungarian background. His father was a minister in the Hungarian Reform Church in various places in the East and in Ohio. Alex knew many languages and after World War II was Publications Procurement Officer with the U.S. Embassy in England where he did much translating. By profession, he was a librarian in the Library of Congress where he met my sister. He said he noticed her for months, but since they had not been properly introduced, he had not spoken to her. But after the introductions and they began dating, new experiences were in store for all of us in the family. Alex's wit and intelligence livened many family dinners. Once when he was in England, we forwarded our family Round

Robin letter to him to read. He responded by writing to us on several sheets of toilet paper.

His love of music was contagious, giving each of us a treat when he played on his baby grand piano or at our house on my father's grand piano. After he gave up playing himself, he spent hours listening to classical music on the radio or from his record collection. Sometimes it almost looked as if he were directing the orchestra when his fingers moved in time with the music.

In his later years, he began painting, and I am the proud owner of a small landscape he created.

In retirement he used his knowledge of languages to teach classes in English to those from other countries. This work, plus other archive-type volunteer work for his church, used much of his time as long as his health held up. But he still had time for a series of beautiful dogs which he and Gertrude trained, fed, and loved.

Thankfully, some of their many travels brought him to visit us. One time he told us that he thought The Wayside, our family home, was the most relaxing place in the world. And he had seen many places of the world but became heartbroken at what happened to his father's native Hungary.

He began to fear that he would not have any grandchildren as his son and daughter did not have children in their early adulthood. But he was overjoyed when he became grandfather to two girls and one boy within a few years. These children, teenagers at the time of his death, will have wonderful memories of their grandfather. I know because I was about that age when I first met my soon-to-be brother-in-law.

I was privileged to take part in the wedding as one of four girls who formed a ribbon aisle for Gertrude to walk through under the apple trees in our lawn in Washington. On their eighth anniversary, Lester and I shared their wedding date. Possibly as a copycat, we also got married on the family lawn, but this one was at our home in Missouri.

When family gathered at Alex's memorial, listening to the beautiful music that he had chosen for this occasion, I remembered with love the music that he brought into our lives with his personality and his talents.

DECORATED FOR CHRISTMAS

During the Thanksgiving season, I received a forwarded e-mail entitled, "Martha Stewart Isn't Coming for Thanksgiving." It reports that since she isn't coming, the writer will not do all those stylish, creative, and elegant things that Martha Stewart talks about. I thoroughly enjoyed it because Martha certainly wasn't coming to our house either. We even used paper plates! Not the flimsy ones. I'm not that uncouth. No, we used the heavy plastic-like ones, in red. They were so good that, much to my daughter-in-law's disgust, I washed a few for future use.

Now at Christmas time, I try a little harder to have a proper festive air. I put up the tree with the help of a seven-year-old great-granddaughter. I brought out all the decorations from various bazaars and gifts from over fifty years of collecting Christmas pretties. The house looked very much like a magazine cover. That is, if you didn't look under things or in the drawers. When I bring out the holiday decorations I am at a loss as to what I should do with all the non-holiday decorations. So I put the Christmas ornaments in front of the usual things in drawers and closets by pushing the everyday stuff to the back. But it looked okay. I wouldn't have been too embarrassed if Martha had dropped by.

Then the weather changed. It snowed. In snowy weather when you live in the country, there is no way to keep the house neat. Shoes and boots are constantly drying over registers or by the fire. Gloves hang over the backs of chairs to dry out between forays into the outside world.

Then there are the coats. A denim chore-type coat needs to be kept handy in case Lester decided to go outside for more wood for the fire. My out-of-style-but-very-warm, pink down-filled coat with a hood is draped over the back of the couch because it is so big that it takes up all the closet room if I put it in the closet. If I leave it in the breezeway closet, it takes half an hour for it to get warm enough to be helpful as a coat. So I leave it over the back of the couch to wear when I walk (slip and slide) up to the mailbox. It is bulky enough that if I did fall I wouldn't break anything because I would be well-padded.

Next are the dressier coats that could be hung up after we come home from town, but since these others are already decorating the couch, there is no reason that these can't join their friends and stay in the living room also.

The festive Christmas sweat shirts also add a seasonal touch as they are scattered around the bedroom, ready for a quick change if we decide to go to town again. They are helpful in hiding the large boxes of Christmas presents still not wrapped. The walkway in our bedroom is lined with these boxes so that a night-time visit to the bathroom can be an exciting adventure since the usual landmarks are hidden behind piles of unwrapped presents.

All of this clutter reminds me of one of the joys of being middle age plus. No one expects things to be perfect because we are 'that age.' We can live in our mess and occasionally see beneath it all to the signs of an up-coming Christmas celebration with the family. The early arrivers might get some of the effect (if the snow has melted by then). But as soon as the first family members arrive and the pre-schoolers start 'examining' everything, the teenagers sprawl on the couches (where they have followed our trend by throwing their coats over the back), and the adults come in with hefty bags full of presents and dishes of food to add to the meal, then all we see is people.

A pre-set table is partially dismantled as we move chairs to allow conversations to begin at the end of the table. The presents under the tree expand to take almost every space that is not being used by the extra tables and extra people. The cats disappear under the beds for a spot of sanctuary and the background music of Christmas carols on my stereo is drowned out by talk and laughter.

That is when I see our house looking its very best for a Merry Christmas. Martha would be envious.

Section Six

A TIME FOR WAR

Dangers, fears, and scary things
Exist within each life,
But wars within our inner selves
Cut sharper than a knife.

CHRISTMAS 1944

Those of us who are old enough have vivid memories of war-time Christmases. One of my memories happened Christmas 1944.

My sister Ellen and I were returning to Washington, D.C. from college in Missouri. We rode the train from Columbia to St. Louis to change trains for the longer trip to Washington. Our old-style coach had windows that opened. The seats were arranged so that each passenger faced the passengers in the next seat. The area behind our backs made an inverted V beneath the tops of the seats that were back to back.

With our pick of the whole car, we settled ourselves midway. After about an hour's wait past the scheduled departure time, the doors swung open and soldiers began entering the car. They were grateful that the train had waited so that they could make connections. Since we were single college girls, we thought the idea of riding with a car full of soldiers sounded great. We learned that the government was trying to get as many service men home for the holidays as possible, and; therefore, the old railway cars had been pressed into service.

We finally rolled out of St. Louis two hours late.

At each stop more soldiers entered, filling up all the seats. Soon there was not even foot room, as one man settled on the floor between us and the two who were facing us. Another rested inside the inverted V behind our seat. One crawled up on the point made by the two seats touching behind us. Finally, the men even began crawling into the luggage rack to find any place to sit or lie down.

Since our train was so late, we had to pull onto sidings often to allow other trains to whisk by. We looked out into the darkness to see brightly lighted Pullman and dining cars speed by while we sat crowded on a siding. I do not remember any complaining, swearing, or struggles over space. Each person was intent on reaching home in time for Christmas. There was very little talking or laughing, and no arguments. The soldiers were bone weary. Most of them just returning from the front.

Ellen and I began to have another problem. Our choice of seats in the middle of the car was a mistake. The restrooms were at each end; the passage from our seats to those restrooms were impossibly blocked with sleeping male bodies.

At one stop some Red Cross women came to the windows to hand in sandwiches and coffee. They were intended for the service men, but our two seat buddies got a sandwich for each of us. We certainly didn't need liquids.

Just as it was getting light, we were put on another siding; we looked out into the faces of steers in a cattle car. Our feeling that we were also herded onto a cattle car faded with the knowledge that our hopes for Christmas and family separated us from the blank looks on the animals' faces.

When it became completely daylight, the two soldiers who had been the first to enter our little section of the car insisted that we make our way down the aisle to the restrooms. It took us nearly thirty minutes to step over and around sleeping soldiers to finally get to the end of the car. As we opened the door to the ladies' room, we found four men inside using the room for a place to sleep. They squeezed themselves into the mass outside until we finished and then returned to use the few feet of space.

When we finally arrived at Harrisburg, Pennsylvania, to transfer trains again, we were thirteen hours late. The car emptied slowly and quietly. Several of the soldiers were met there, and we witnessed some of our friends of the night joyously greeting family. Most, like us, were going on farther, but we all quickly found our way to restrooms, telephones, drinking fountains, and snack bars.

The memory of those polite, weary soldiers and their concern for two college girls who shared their space as we headed home for Christmas remains a great gift. We learned that discomfort is not important if it helps us reach our goal.

Merry Christmas to all who share in a journey to Christmas.

HUGS CAN'T BE SENT ON THE TELEPHONE

When you reach middle age plus, some sounds and activities trigger a vivid memory even when you don't know why this happens. Yesterday my son called me from his new home in Milwaukee. Since he had been just thirty miles up the road at Butler through all of his married life, most of our telephone conversations in recent years had been just quick messages about when he would be down or when one of his sons was going to be playing ball or wrestling. But this call was different since he was much farther away, and we had no immediate plans to get together very soon. At the end of the call my memory flew back to the call I received from him during the Vietnam War.

Toward the end of the 'conflict,' Michael was drafted and trained as a medic. We hoped he would be assigned to an army hospital somewhere in the United States, but that was not going to be what happened.

I was at my desk in the Welfare Office (that was the term then) in Butler when I got a call from California. It was Michael telling me that he was going to be sent to Vietnam very soon. I knew this would be a possibility but had blocked the thought from my mind with hopes that it wouldn't happen. When the news did come, I couldn't think of anything to say to this son who was going to face unknown dangers in an unknown country. I said something stupid like, "I was hoping you would stay here," and he repeated the news that he was to be sent to Vietnam. There were long pauses in our talk as I tried not to let my emotions show, and he couldn't tell me anything else. He finally said others were waiting to use the phone, and to tell Dad, Susan (his youngest sister), and the others goodbye. Then he was gone.

I sat there at my desk in a busy office realizing I had let a precious moment go by. I was talking to my son for maybe the last time. I hadn't told him how proud we were of him or how much we loved him. I let him go with stupid remarks about useless hopes and disappointments that he had no control over.

After I had a quiet cry at my desk, I picked up the phone again to tell Lester the news.

Obviously, Michael did come home from Vietnam. He established a family and has a good job that unfortunately sent him farther away from us than I would wish. But he is well, safe, and still calls to give us any news.

His telephone call brought back the memory of that other difficult call years ago. The pleasant talk about his job, his family, the weather, and possible summer plans for a float trip with his brother and nephew were a far cry from the dire news he gave me on that day thirty years ago. Why did that other conversation pop into my memory so quickly after we hung up?

Even though there is no danger in his present situation and I can pick up the phone and call him anytime I want, or get in the car to drive to see him, I again let another opportunity go by without telling him how important he is to us. Once more, I didn't tell him the things on my heart but kept the conversation on news and events.

It is easy to understand why this happens. My parents were of the generation that didn't show emotions. My mother's words of comfort or love were cloaked in assurances that everything would be all right, or I would feel better in the morning. In our family we were proud of each other and enjoyed being together, but rarely did we speak of our deeper feelings. Like mother, like daughter, I inherited that tendency. My late brother, Ralph, talked about this with me shortly before he died. He said that his children had taught him to start expressing his love in person. We had all been able to put the words on paper but rarely said them. With Ralph's advice, I started being more verbal with my emotions. Because as we found out in the unexpected sudden illness that took our brother's life, we don't know when we will have other opportunities.

I think I'll call Michael again today. We won't talk about the weather.

206 For Everything There Is a Season

RATIONED SHOES

I find it hard to buy shoes. I get a pair that fits me fine, but in a few weeks when the new has worn off, they are too short. I was once told that I have a flexible arch, whatever that means. I end up with pairs of shoes under the bed with nothing that feels good to wear.

I don't worry too much about this problem, because I can remember so vividly the much greater problem of buying shoes when I was a teenager in the middle of World War II. Shoes were rationed to two pairs per person per year. When we bought our shoes, we had to present a ration ticket along with the money. For a teenage girl this was hard because I needed school shoes, dress shoes, and outside work shoes, plus all the other appealing shoes I saw in the stores.

My father did not use all his ration tickets since he wore one pair of white shoes in the summer and one pair of black shoes in the winter. Since he did not wear out a pair each year, he had plenty of old shoes to serve as his work shoes. He had one ration ticket to spare. The problem began when he had to decide which daughter would get it.

Sometimes shoe stores received a shipment of

canvas shoes made of composition soles with no leather or much of anything else in them. We could buy them without a ration ticket. Even though they usually lasted only about a month before falling apart, we bought them because it was a luxury to have one more pair.

I look at young people today wearing their sport shoes that we used to call tennis shoes. When I was young, only really poor children wore tennis shoes for anything but sports. In the winter, children wore only oxfords or work shoes of some sort to school. In my experience, children never wore cowboy boots to school either, but I'm sure that varied in different parts of the country.

The ankle-high sports shoes, like running shoes, that all kids now wear to almost every occasion make their feet look extremely large, especially when they are wearing shorts and leave the shoestrings untied. But I am glad they have shoes that make them feel good about themselves. I hope the family can afford them.

Today when I watch young women and older teen girls at church and other dress-up times, I realize that the shoes they are wearing are the kind that I had considered 'old women's shoes.' Now that I am middle age plus, I still think they look like old women's shoes. I won't wear them.

In spite of rationing, cost, style, and fit, I am happiest when I can use my favorite type of footgear. I've never had to pay a high price, give a ration ticket, or abandon them under the bed. Just let me go bare-footed!

IT'S HARD TO REJOICE

In spite of the glory of spring, with the beginnings of flowers, humming birds returning, and young animal and fowl being born, it has been hard to rejoice this week. The tragedies around the world make us want to weep for the hatred that continues to surface in the human race. Those of us who are middle age plus lived through the Nazi hatred, but we didn't really know all that was going on until after the war was over.

Today we see the lines of refugees streaming into the countries that are not able to care for them, and we realize that these folk look just like we do. We had become calloused to seeing the human tragedies in parts of Africa, and we are saddened but not as personally affected as we are now with the same thing happening in what most of us remember as Yugoslavia. Then in beautiful Colorado we see high school students that could easily pass for any of our students here at home being forever traumatized by the hatred and violence of fellow students. And we weep. As the black father who lost a son reaches for the hand of a blond student who lost his sister and witnessed the death of the man's son, we sob in sympathy. Yet we rejoice that the blond youth responded to the hand clasp in appreciation.

As these hands of different colors express love and acceptance, we realize that all the tragedies that happen in our world to people of any color are equally terrible. Those in our vicinity affect us more, but no matter where they occur, lives are destroyed, hearts broken and hopes shattered.

It is not humanly possible to grieve for each of the atrocities that go on daily in the world. Since we are now 'blessed' with instant communication from all over the earth (and beyond), we are constantly bombarded. We could be in a constant state of shock if we allowed ourselves to react equally to each story.

I am immensely saddened by each of the events this spring, but it would double the effects of the tragedies if we could not look beyond them to find hope and joy in the good things that are also happening this season. After all, one of the advantages of being middle age plus is that we have successfully reached this age. We have survived wars, droughts, depressions, floods, unemployment, family problems, and sickness. But we are still here. So, I will follow the poet A.E. Housman who writes, "About the woodlands I will go/ To see the cherry hung with snow." He expresses his philosophy as a young man of twenty feeling that the fifty years he has left to live is not enough time to really appreciate the glories of spring. I have passed my "three score years and ten" that he mentions, but I expect to have a good many more springs. Just in case, however, I don't want to miss a day of this one.

I spent hours waiting for the five goslings to hatch and leave their nest last week, and rejoiced when I was able to see the last little ball of fuzz drop from the elevated nest into the pond to join his parents and siblings. I walked the lawn to check on the survival of each tree and shrub planted last year, finding only one that did not survive the winter. I sat on our deck and traced a robin's flight to figure out where her nest is located. And I finally mastered the steps it takes to receive and send e-mail messages. (Whoops, that has nothing to do with spring, but it has been a cause for celebration for me.)

Another reason for celebrating this spring is the chiggers haven't returned. Or, if they have, they have not found me yet!

I'D RATHER DRIVE

Risks and dangers are always a possibility when you start on a trip, but in spite of road hazzards, when I travel I prefer to drive if possible. I am not afraid of flying; I just like the feeling of being in control of my schedule when I drive. A recent trip to Shreveport, Louisiana, almost changed my mind until I arrived and heard the horror stories of those who had flown to the meeting.

My trip started out great with a rather leisurely drive down to Ft. Smith, Arkansas, the afternoon before the meeting was to begin. I was traveling scenic U.S. 71, a twisty, two lane road through the Ozarks. I decided to stop for overnight at Ft. Smith rather than drive on to a stop closer to my next day's meeting.

I found an inexpensive motel and thought I was all set for a relaxing evening of eating and watching television alone in my second story motel room. I began doing just that when the television started flashing warnings about a tornado watch for a certain county. I didn't know what county I was in and the map was in the car. Since it had started raining quite hard, and I didn't want to go get the map, I kept watching for a map on television.

Fairly soon the reports became more specific with Ft. Smith mentioned as in the middle of this watch. Along with this announcement came all the dire warnings of what not to do. One was, don't remain in an upstairs room, and stay away from large windows. Another was, don't go outside. Okay. Here I was in a second floor motel room with a large plate glass window on the southwest corner of the building. The lobby of the motel was on the other side and was very small and also glass-covered. If I went out into the storm, in addition to getting wet, I'd be putting myself at more risk. I wasn't sure that the lobby would be any safer. Since the report also warned against staying in cars, the option of sitting in my car was no good either.

I decided not to worry since watches didn't mean a tornado was coming to this exact spot. So I closed the drapes and continued to watch television. Within minutes tornado sirens began blowing. There must have been one immediately above my room from the sound of it. The television pinpointed where the tornado had been sighted—at the intersection of Highway 71 and some lettered, county road. This was not very comforting as I was half a block off of Highway 71 but had no idea what lettered roads were nearby.

Other directions continued on television about what to do. One said to go into a small room or closet with no windows if no other safe place was available. I went into the bathroom and sat, you know where, with the door open a crack to watch and listen to directions from the television. Suddenly it went blank while the sirens continued to blow for almost twenty minutes. When they finally quieted down, I looked outside and saw my car still sitting undamaged and no visible signs of damage nearby. I went to bed and actually did go to sleep.

The next morning I started quite early without eating any breakfast, thinking I would stop later for a break. The morning was lovely with freshly washed trees shining in the sun. I was enjoying my drive when I came to a long line of trucks and cars stopped ahead of me. Naturally, I also stopped thinking it was one-way traffic due to road repairs. It was early for workers to be about, but perhaps the hot weather caused them to work early. After I sat there for at least ten minutes, the man in the truck ahead of me walked up the line to see what was going on. He reported that an eighteen-wheeler loaded with gasoline had turned over. Fuel was spilling out, and they would not let anyone by for quite a while. As I pondered what 'quite a while' might mean, cars ahead of me in the line began turning around. One driver stopped long enough to yell that it would be at least three hours before anyone could get through. Since I didn't want to sit for three hours in the middle of a scenic woods with no breakfast, I too turned around. I took the first road going west and driving by instinct I headed west, then south, and finally back east again rejoining Highway 71 and on down to Shreveport.

Many of the women who were scheduled to be at the meeting had not arrived. They had flown. The same storm that went over Ft. Smith had delayed their flights. Some had to stay overnight in an unscheduled stop and others arrived as much as twelve hours late. One woman never did get her luggage that didn't keep up with all the different flights they put her on.

My experience, though somewhat scary, was thought provoking. Their's was also sobering as well as frustrating because they had to depend on someone else to decide what would happen to them. I had to alter my planned route, but I was able to take control myself. I prefer that.

I did realize that if I am going to be blown away in the night, I want to be blown away from home or at least from a place I know. The thought of being an unidentified body somewhere in Arkansas did not appeal to me!

THE BOOGIE MAN
WILL GET YOU

Worries about dire happenings such as the Y2K bug threat make me think back over the three quarters of a century that I have lived to remember all the other 'scares' that we have experienced.

I believe the first time I was ever aware of something on the national scene that frightened me was when the Lindberg baby was kidnaped. Since I was quite small, the idea that someone could enter my bedroom window and take me away from my family was terrifying. My mother was of the school that believed that no matter how cold it was outside, we should sleep with our windows open. As I lay in bed watching the curtains blowing, I imagined I saw someone lurking on the porch roof that was just beyond the window. I slept next to the wall in the bed I shared with my sister. Ellen told me she was too old for kidnappers to take, but I was the right age. Of course, that added to my fears, but I consoled myself that since she slept on the outside, the kidnappers would get her first.

My high school years were in war-time Washington, D.C. where there was more of a sense of readiness for problems relating to the war than I experienced on our summers back on the farm in Missouri. We put blackout shades on every window, we did not show outside lights, we could not use our car for recreational purposes, and at school I was in charge of getting all the students out of one hall on the third floor when we had an air-raid drill. There was no feeling of panic, but every high school boy knew that immediately upon graduation he would be drafted. Instead of having pep rallies, we had savings bond rallies to help the war effort.

Years later, after the end of World War II, we experienced the years of the Cold War. By then I was a mother. We wondered what fate was in store for our children as we debated about the pros and cons of bomb shelters and how to provide for life after a possible Atomic Bomb attack. The movie, The Day After, that was located in Lawrence, Kansas, made the possibilities seem even more real when we heard our neighboring towns named in this fictional account of an attack in our area.

We lived in several different towns in western Missouri during this time, far from the nation's capitol where I spent the war years. Then, our mid-western home was a possible target because of the missile silos spread throughout the area. One was a few miles west of our parsonage in Archie, Missouri. We passed several others whenever we drove any distance.

Another threat that is constantly with us in this area is the possibility of tornadoes hitting. Now that we live in a converted modular home that fear is possibly more real than when we lived in a home with a basement.

Terrorism, road rage, senseless violence in

crowded places, traffic accidents, falls, and deadly illnesses all loom constantly on the horizon. With our
instant news media which eagerly awaits an opportunity to play up some frightening event, not many days
go by but what we are made aware of some new threat
to our well-being. Much of what we read today cau-
tions us to be careful about the foods we eat, the things
we touch, the air we breath, the water we drink, and
the people we associate with. We could easily become
a nations of hermits living as recluses away from all
these dangers.

When looking back at my years in the twentieth
century, I smile when I remember the attention we
gave to each of these threats. If it hadn't been so serious I could laugh at the preparations that we made to
protect ourselves from the possible dangers. The shelters designed to protect us from an atomic blast would
have been useless. We now have better knowledge of
the power of nuclear explosions. Sleeping next to the
wall would not really have protected me from the evil
kidnapper of my childhood imagination. And even
though the World War II threats to Washington were
a very real possibility, they did not occur. I lived as
happy a teen-age existence as any skinny, straight-
haired girl could expect.

So when 1999 bowed out, I was awake to experience the beginning of a new age. I did not ruin the day
by imagining what might occur. My life shows that
most of what we fear does not happen. If it does, then
holding on to the pleasure of living happy hours, days,
or years instead of worrying about some future problem will more than compensate.

But maybe it would be best not to leave your window open for those kidnappers.

THE CLUMSIEST CHILD
IN THE CLASS

The beginning of school brings back a vivid traumatic memory of school. I attended a large elementary school in Washington, D.C. with three floors.

The incident I recall happened in Miss Ward's fourth grade. I had a very good education in the public schools in Washington, but the fourth grade was not one of the highlights. Miss Ward used lots of make-up and dyed her hair red (so obviously dyed that even fourth graders could tell). Ellen had been in her class a few years earlier and Miss Ward thought I didn't measure up to my sister.

For some reason, one day she asked me, all by myself, to take the large fish bowl down to the girls' restroom, clean it out, refill it, and bring it back to the classroom.

Since our classroom was on the third floor, I had to carry the bowl through swinging doors, down two flights of stairs, through another set of swinging doors, into the girls' playroom, and finally into the restroom. Two fish, two turtles, and some snails lived in this bowl which was lined with beautiful marbles and colored gravel.

I got the bowl clean after putting the fish and turtles in another sink while I washed out the classroom bowl. I washed the gravel and the marbles, then refilled the bowl part so the turtles could stay above water until I got back to the classroom where there was an island contraption that fit in the middle of the bowl. Feeling proud of myself, I started back up the two flights of stairs with the cleaned fish bowl and its inhabitants.

Then the bell rang for recess for the lower grades. The stairs immediately swarmed with children from grades one to three. Intent on getting outside to play, they didn't notice me standing there with wet hands, a wet fish bowl, and no place to escape. As you guessed, the bowl slipped from my grasp. The marbles merrily bounded down the metal stairs as I stood in the water amid the broken glass holding on to the two turtles which I rescued from the steps. The fish flopped around a step or two lower.

The kindergarten teacher, hearing the noise of two dozen marbles clinking down the stairs, came to my rescue. She picked up the fish and herded the children around the mess while trying to console me for the accident.

Miss Ward arrived and said, "I should have known better than to send you. You're the clumsiest child in the class!"

I don't know if I was the clumsiest one or not. I know I felt that I was at that moment. And I agreed. She shouldn't have sent any fourth grader on such an errand.

I still feel the sting of those remarks accompanied by the sound of marbles bouncing down the stairs.

FEAR OF HEIGHTS

I am moderately afraid of heights. Some of my worst dreams involve falling. I avoid roads that bring the driver near the edge of a precipice. If there is a little level ground between me and the drop-off, I do fine. But I don't even like to see someone else standing on the very edge of a cliff. When I am with children, I nearly cut off the circulation in their hands, holding them tightly to be sure they go nowhere near the edge of any mountain or ledge.

I think this started when I was very small and two uncles flew into our pasture in an open cockpit plane. They took turns taking all their nieces and nephews up in the rear seat of this barn-stormer type plane. I was sent up with my brothers, Ralph and Vernon, who spent the entire flight pretending to throw me out of the plane.

My visit to the Arch in St. Louis was great until I tried to use the viewing platform where you lean across a firm structure to look straight down through a window. My head began to swirl. I had to get away from the windows. I was very eager to get in the elevator seat to go back to earth.

I rejoiced recently when I heard that the bridge

over the Missouri River at Boonville had been replaced. When we used to drive to Central Methodist College at Fayette, our route took us over this chain-link, floored bridge high above the river. The vibrations of the car as the tires reacted to the unusual flooring, plus the height of the bridge, made this a nightmare for me. If I was not driving, I shut my eyes. That didn't work too well if I was at the wheel. So I gritted my teeth and took deep breaths.

I awoke this morning after having one of my bad dreams about heights. I was still very caught up in the horror of the dream while I dressed for the day. As I started to walk away from the bedside where I was dressing, I suddenly tripped and fell forward. Catching myself on some furniture, I looked to see what had tripped me. The end of my shoestring had caught in the grill over the vent of the furnace, stopping that foot in its tracks. Remembering my dream, I had to laugh that my fear of a dramatic fall from some high spot had never happened, but here in my bedroom a simple shoestring could have caused a serious injury.

I remembered another time when I went outside to get something out of the car and my toe caught in the hem of my bathrobe making me fall off the deck out onto the frozen lawn.

Neither event caused me any physical problem, but each made me realize the truth. The big things we fear probably will never happen. But a loose shoestring or a comfy housecoat can bring us to our knees in a hurry. There must be a moral here somewhere.

LIGHTS OUT!

Winter has its hazards. No matter how neat a house looks in good weather, as soon as it begins to snow, the home begins to look like a refugee camp. A recent storm made the problem more pronounced in our area because we were without electricity for three different times during the ice storm. The third time we were without electricity for over sixteen hours.

Bringing out makeshift equipment for heating and lighting, adding more clothes for warmth, not having the use of the clothes dryer, the hot water heater, the microwave, and the amusement of the television or computer brought back memories of the past that many of us had not thought of lately. The big difference was that in 'the olden days' that was the usual way to live. We were prepared for it. Then, we did not miss the modern conveniences because we didn't know about them.

Trying to recreate those days unexpectedly was not easy to do. Each time I went into a darkened room, I automatically switched on the light switch, even though I was going after the kerosene lamp. I picked up the cordless phone to use and in a panic thought the phone lines were also down. Then I remembered that the base unit ran by electricity.

When we got the lamp lit, we were both surprised at how dim the light was. Surely the lamps of our childhood put out more light than that! It took some scrambling to find (in the dark) a battery operated radio so we could keep current on what the weather was going to do next. It is surprising how attuned we are to hearing the five, six, and ten o'clock news and weather.

Since our home is off the public road and the windows were iced up, we couldn't even see how the neighbors were faring until we used the phone. Then because of our common emergency needs, we caught up on neighborhood news that we had not heard during the holidays when we were all involved in our own family celebrations.

We were lucky that our cook stove is gas, even though we had to use a match to light the burners. Since our oven is electric, we cooked everything on the burners. We left them on for added heat in the room.

Our great-granddaughter got a lesson on how many things are operated by electricity. She said she could play her kindergarten computer game because she didn't mind being in a dark room! She also had her first experience of a bath and hair wash in a bathtub with water heated on the stove and carried in to add to the cold water. For some reason she didn't play in the tub as much as she often does.

Our heartfelt thanks go out to those poor workers who had to spend those sixteen hours looking for the cause of our outage. They didn't even have the minor comforts that we had in our home, but they helped us see the light again. And that lighted our

way to memories of long, dim winter nights that always made everyone very glad when spring came.

One of the worst things about the storm was that
the clouds and snow blocked out one of the best lights
we have--a full moon.

DANGER IN THE WATER

We have a small lake or a big pond right by our house. I call it a lake when I want to impress people, but it really is a pond. Its color has given us the name for our homestead, Bronze Pond. When I am feeling stressed out all I need to do is go sit on the deck by the pond and watch the reflections of the trees shimmering in the water when the wind blows. A leisurely canoe trip a time or two around the pond (with someone else doing the paddling) is even more relaxing. Lying on an inflated mattress while floating on the water is a real luxury--until I need to get out. Then avoiding muddy footing underneath can be a problem. On the whole I'd say our pond is worth all the tranquilizers on the market for reducing stress and helping us enjoy God's world.

That is, until we really look closely at God's world. Right now the pond is a little lower than usual due to the dry weather. The water is very clear recently because there have been no rains to bring extra water in to stir it up. None of our children have been swimming lately to cause the mud bottom to cloud the water. I can sit on the deck and see what is going on underneath the beautiful reflections on top.

The middle-sized bass seem to have formed a partnership arrangement where they float about eight inches apart from each other as they come closer and closer to the shore line. There is no motion in the water and very little sign of movement underneath, but they will glide into water only inches deep where the tiny minnow and little fish live. Suddenly one of the bass will strike at an unsuspecting little fish, which, of course, stirs up all the other nearby small fry. The two bass have lunch (or supper depending on the hour).

This activity goes on by the hour as I sit watching. Then I realize that these bass are concentrating on this shallow area of the pond because if they went out deeper, then they would be a meal for some of the yet bigger fish out there.

When we take heels of bread out to feed the fish, we always put some crumbs near the shore for the babies, and throw more out toward the end of the dock. I know it doesn't work, but I keep thinking that if I feed the bigger fish out there they will leave the little ones alone. We have bought some floating fish food that Lester throws way out into the pond hoping the catfish will grow bigger to replace some we lost a few years ago. We also drop some in the shallow water for the small ones to work on. The pellets are too large for them to swallow, but they keep working at them until they dissolve enough for them to eat.

I have a rule for our family, or anyone who fishes here. They cannot fish from our dock. I think it would be dirty pool to try to catch fish where they have become used to being fed. Our son fishes from the canoe and usually catches five or six in each outing, but he throws them back in to grow bigger or catch again another day.

I have been told that fish don't feel pain, but how do we know? I can't imagine any living creature that has a hook in its mouth not feeling it. One time I had a fishing lure hit me on the side of the head as I was dangling my feet over the back of a john boat. I can attest that I did indeed feel it, but then I am not a fish.

In addition to the hazards to our pond's population—people fishing, bigger fish, and turtles—we also have frequent visits from a wading heron who quietly and very slowly walks the shore line until its curved neck suddenly strikes out. We see a fish momentarily in the beak before it is swallowed. This seemingly awkward creature can move with extreme grace and quickness which is a beauty to behold. But hard on the fish.

As one of God's creatures on this earth, I can say that I am thankful that our species is usually not in danger of being eaten by another. I can sit to enjoy the picture presented by our pond and remain tranquil, even if I feel sorry for the fish.

Now when using a moment by the pond to relax, I will try to avoid watching the feeding processes going on under the water. I doubt that I would have become middle age plus if I had been born a fish.

Section Seven

A TIME FOR PEACE

A restful scene, a thoughtful word
A gentle April rain
Are all we need to calm our fear
Or ease our hidden pain.

A HOST OF
GOLDEN DAFFODILS

Driving around the county, I passed a lovely hill-top where there were some old cedar trees, a couple of shade trees, an old rusty pump still in the ground, and hundreds of blooming daffodils. The place obviously had been a home site in years past, but there were no remains of any buildings, signs of a driveway or any left-behind machines or trash. Just a beautiful spot, made more beautiful by the abundant blooms.

I couldn't help thinking about the woman (it must have been a woman) who planted all these bulbs. Did she plant just a few and the years allowed mother nature to reproduce these hundreds of plants? Or did she separate the bulbs each year to create the massive display? I pictured her standing on this beautiful hillside looking out at the view that stretched for miles, and then looking down at the golden display of flowers at her feet. I hope it gave her pleasure to see the results of her work. Perhaps there were other flowers when she lived on this hillside. Maybe other seasons will display even more beauty. But the day I passed there were only the budding trees, the cedars, and rows and rows of daffodils.

Maybe she sat among these blooms with her children and shared a picnic lunch. Or maybe she and her husband sat out there on a warm, early spring evening after the work was done and relaxed in the midst of this glory.

Or was this a cry for beauty from a woman who had her hours so filled with drudgery that she had little time for the nicer things in life? I doubt that I will ever know. As I came home and saw my own attempts at starting daffodils in our yard, I gave thanks to the hundreds of women and men who have left some mark of beauty where they once passed.

Occasionally there will be flowers blooming by the roadside where someone must have planted them there for passers-by to enjoy. Hundreds of daylilies will greet us in a few weeks along many roads. We wonder if they were planted, or if the road grader displaced some bulbs from another spot and left them to multiply in the ditches and highway right-of-ways. Either way, I enjoy seeing them each year.

Since I have reached middle age plus, I wonder how I will be remembered. Maybe even long after no one can remember who I was, there will remain a glimpse of beauty where one of my attempts at gardening left a flower. Maybe a great-great-great-grandchild will see a picture of me and remember that I was the one who loved redbud trees, daffodils, and forsythia each spring. Or if she doesn't know anything about me, maybe she will have inherited that love of these early flowers, not knowing she shared it with an early ancestor.

I cherish a picture of my mother in her lawn with our daughter. They are looking at a daffodil. That daughter is now a grandmother and shares this same lawn with her grandchild. When they enjoy these flowers together, I am sure that somewhere in eternity there is a smile.

I hope that a smile was also shared by the unknown woman who once lived on the lovely hillside where I enjoyed the spot of beauty she created years before.

LOOKING AT THINGS IN A DIFFERENT LIGHT

In spite of the very dry summer I was in hopes of seeing some pretty fall colors last weekend as I drove through the northern Ozarks. Since I was heading east in the morning, the rising sun and heavy fog kept me from seeing much more than the lines on the road ahead of me while concentrating on my driving. As I passed Truman Lake, I looked for color on the opposite banks but was disappointed to see only some dark reds among the many green cedars.

On the way home at the end of the day, I again found myself facing the sun. Without the fog, I could see much better but still couldn't find the beauty I hoped for. One particular spot on the road had always lifted my spirits. The highway rises from crossing an arm of the lake before passing between two rock cliffs chiseled out to make the road. Above the rocky sides there are many varieties of trees. In the spring this area is abundant with dogwood and redbud. Usually in the fall, the scene shines with reds, yellows, and oranges.

236 For Everything There Is a Season

But last weekend I felt sad as I approached this view and saw no brilliance at all in the foliage. Distracted from my driving a bit while I searched for more color, I was startled to hear a truck behind me. I glanced into the rearview mirror to locate the sound. In addition to a farm truck with a bad muffler, I was amazed to see the very scene I had been hoping to see on this hill reflected in my mirror.

The light from the lowering sun was shining directly on the trees along the eastern bank of the lake that I had just crossed. Every warm color imaginable was highlighted in the sun and punctuated by the deep greens of the cedars. I slowed to let the truck pass and to enjoy this reflected view as long as possible.

During the rest of the trip home I kept my eyes fixed on the rearview mirror to see the same phenomenon repeated time after time.

The experience was much like our lives. We travel through with one point of view and often miss the grandeur each of our lives offers if we look with a new perspective. Seeing things in a different light can give golden overtones to a drab day.

As we reach middle age plus, we find ourselves looking back more often than in earlier years. Often we discover that many of the times that have passed were more meaningful and beautiful than we realized while experiencing them. Putting the light of advancing age into our memories brings out the highlights with clarity. At the time, with our eyes straight ahead, intent on the responsibilities of the day and the path we needed to follow, we allowed little time for the luxury of stopping to see what other views might bring.

When I had traveled this same road in the past, my time schedule was different. I drove west in the morning with the rising sun at my back, giving me every benefit of direct sunlight on the trees I was approaching. This trip reversed the process, making me think that there was no color.

This insight is worth as much as the glory of the changing leaves. I realize that I must take time to look at things in various lights. I will still try to keep my eyes on the road and be watchful for what is ahead, but I won't neglect the scene from the rearview mirror.

I will go sit on the deck now to enjoy the trees right here in our own yard. The sun has just come out from behind the clouds, and I hear a squirrel barking in the front lawn. I will look at them from every direction.

SUNLIGHT REFLECTED IN OUR FLOWERS

Each autumn I renew my love affair with a yellow weed I call Spanish blossom. Others have given it different names, but it is the brilliant yellow flower that blooms in the fields and along any unmowed road. The abundance of this flower is part of its appeal, but the tenacity of the plant is also inspiring. If the plants are allowed to grow, they will reach three or four feet in height with dozens of small sunflower-like blooms at the top. But if they are mowed off, there will still be small plants with smaller blooms appearing a week or so after the mower passes. No matter what happens, they are determined to produce this cheery flower for the world to see.

The yellows and golds of the fall give us our 'fix' of beauty to carry us through the winter until the spring greets us again with early yellow or gold flowers. This profuse abundance of color affects me as a promise of all the glories that our life offers us. We don't go many months without this reflected sunlight shown in our flowers. I will relish each day that we can enjoy the brightness of fall, both in the skies and on the ground.

We had an exceptionally long and hot summer which lasted later into September than usual, so maybe we will have an exceptionally long and mild autumn to follow it. Probably not, since this is Missouri with its unpredictable weather. But the uncertainty of the time left to enjoy these blooms makes them even more special.

Perhaps it is this same emotion that makes this middle age plus time of life also special. Since we aren't sure how much longer we will be able to produce our blossoms or enjoy those that come from other people, we try to make the most of each glorious moment.

I can divide these moments into two main parts. First, those I experience each day, such as driving down a country road that is bordered by my yellow friends. Second, the memories of meaningful times in the past that linger in my mind just as the images of these flowers stay with me through the winter. Neither would be complete by itself. I need the stimulation of everyday activities to allow me to continue to be productive and useful. But I also need the memories of those things and people that are no longer with us to help me keep my own life in perspective. I can learn from those memories and be nourished by them. I am also aware that I may be creating memories for others to keep in their minds as they reach this stage. That really keeps me on my toes.

I know that some of the memories I leave behind me are not good ones for those who will remember them. Just as each of these yellow flowers is not absolutely perfect, for many have blemishes or broken petals. The overall effect is great. My hope for the memories I leave behind is that even if some are flawed or tarnished, maybe the overall effect will be helpful or pleasant.

When I finish writing this, I will get on our riding mower to mow the lawn at The Wayside, my home place. As I ride through the field of beautiful blossoms to reach this lawn, I will glory in each moment and in each flower, and try not to think about the chiggers I will probably get from being out in the weeds.

THERE'S GOLD IN THEM THAR FIELDS

I am trying very hard to keep from writing about how much I love the brilliant yellow Spanish blossoms that are in every field and roadside this month. Each fall I have found some way to highlight these beauties in at least one of my columns. I have decided not to impose my extreme fondness for this plant on you readers again this year.

Instead of mentioning how this cheery flower lifts my spirits each time I turn a corner past a different field and see yet another abundant display, I will write instead about something else.

I won't reminisce with you about my first memory of these flowers when I was in my early teens as I raced our saddle horse, Princess Peggy, through a field covered with the yellow blooms. I will refrain from relating how my sister and I, with friends, used to take the family car and aimlessly drive up and down country roads in our county and over into Kansas just to see more of the abundant color. I'm not even going to brag that the beauty this flower brings our county this time of year equals the fall colors presented by the trees in the Ozarks.

No, I will choose other topics this season. My loyal readers have already heard each year about my love affair with this plant. Enough is enough.

Instead I am going to write about our cats. Wynkum and Blynkum, the pure white siblings, are getting a little on the heavier side now that they are past the ten-year mark. Their kissing cousin, pure black Nod, is still sleek and slinky, but she is beginning to sprout a few white hairs in her fur to show her age.

Along with us, our pets have reached middle age plus. But also along with us, they are enjoying themselves very much in this time of their lies.

Since they are outdoor cats (except when I happen to let them inside daily), they love to roam the fields. The two white cats stand out like corner posts as they go hunting through the beautiful yellow Spanish blossoms. Nod's black coat makes a startling contrast to the gold around her as she also ventures into the fields. I think they are enjoying this season as much as we are by their eagerness to roam in the flowers.

Nod is waiting on the shelf of the deck for me each morning as I wake up. She seems to know when I will be up and about, as she patiently waits for me to open the door. She goes immediately to the cabinet where I keep the cat food and purrs and rubs and meows, depending on my speed in tending to her, until I select a can and go out the rear door to feed her in 'their room.'

We have a glass-enclosed back porch with a swinging cat door for the three cats to have security from strays and dogs. There they are equipped with pillows, a heat lamp with a thermostat, and food dishes.

We don't need to water them because of our lawn-side pond taking care of that chore.

Blynkum usually has appeared at the back door by the time I get the food to the cats' room, but if Wynkum comes, he wants no part of the canned food. He wants to come inside and be served a bowl of milk in the kitchen. Then he will find the softest spot in the house and sleep off the effects of his nightly adventures. If he can sleep on the bed, that is fine, but if there is a folded blanket at the foot of the bed, he prefers to lie on that, unless he chooses the spot between the two pillows. The other two cats will sometimes ask to come inside again, or, if Lester is out and about, Nod will follow him as he works just as a dog would.

Of course, we don't spoil our cats. They have to earn their keep by killing numerous rats and mice. We know they do because they bring them to the door and leave them there for us to step on when we go outside in the dim morning light.

Now that I have told you more than you wanted to know about our pets, would you rather I had written about the beautiful Spanish blossoms?

THE QUIETER JOYS OF WINTER

A few weeks ago I was resisting signs of winter coming. The leaves were beautiful and the sun so bright that I wanted no suggestion that this was going to pass. I even drove around taking pictures of some particularly beautiful trees. We enjoyed the beauty of a shapely and brilliantly colored tree out in a pasture all by itself. We pictured how nice that tree would look at our place. Our own oaks were more colorful this year than usual, and on sunny days they nearly rivaled the hard maples.

But rains came, and the winds blew. The weather turned colder and grayer. There would be very few days of color left. Surprisingly, I didn't grieve. Perhaps, because the passing of warm days coincided with the end of our remodeling work, I was ready to relax indoors and enjoy the rarity of a completely clean house (well, more than usual, anyway!).

Today we have a wood fire in our free-standing fireplace that Lester calls a stove. I have a CD of romantic music playing, which replaces the country/rock that one of the carpenters played constantly. I have a stack of unread magazine I will read when I have more energy. Right now I am happy to look out at the gray skies, enjoy the fire and music, and rejoice that I don't have a single floor to mop or shelf to dust.

The coming of winter releases responsibilities that warm weather brings with it. For instance, I will not have to mow the lawn each week for a long time. Even though I won't have flowers to enjoy, I will not have the worry of weeding them either. Since our oaks don't drop their leaves until spring, I won't even have the nagging feeling that I should get out and rake the lawn.

I have completely enjoyed spring, summer, and fall, but now it is almost winter. I think I am ready.

So it is with my life. I am not quite in the winter of my life yet, though I can certainly see the signs. The burst of life, growth, and energy of my spring-time matured into productive years of summer and the harvest of fall. Now that fall is nearly over in my life, as well as in this year, I find I am ready to enjoy the quieter joys of winter.

One of the best things about winter, and older age, is it gives me lots of excuses to get out of tasks I'd rather not do. It's too cold today. I will wait for a better day for this chore. Or, I'd like to go to that meeting, but since the forecast is for snow, I'd better stay home.

Having lived quite a few years, I realize that it isn't important if everything gets done perfectly. My neighbor, who is famous for her cooking, has even decided that it is okay to use frozen, pre-prepared pie crusts. Another middle age plus friend gave up making her bed daily because no one saw it anyway. It was wasted motion.

My biggest concession to increasing age probably is in entertaining. I used to get out all my good silver and dishes to have everything matched up with nap-kins, centerpiece, and dishes all coordinated. The other day when I was hostess to a club meeting, I used su-permarket paper napkins, a centerpiece I won as a door prize last month, two different kinds of dishes, and stainless steel silverware from three different sets. No one ran screaming from the house. All said they had a good time.

It is in the winters of life, or seasons, we become more laid back and relaxed and can spend time goof-ing off without feeling guilty.

I will get a renewed burst of energy in the spring, but for now, just picture me in a cozy chair with my feet up, feeling happy that I have reached this season of relaxation.

SONGS THROUGH
THE YEARS

All week I have been thinking about April showers, and remembering the strong, deep voice of Al
Jolson singing, "When April showers may come your
way, They'll bring the flowers that bloom in May, So
just keep looking for the bluebird and listening for his
song, Whenever April showers come along." Such songs
take me back in time and brighten my mood immediately. When I listen to some of the current songs, I
wonder about their mood-setting abilities. Obviously,
many people will remember and cherish them, just as
I do the songs from my growing-up years. But it is
hard for us older folk to understand how the loud rep-
etition of the same phrase could become a nostalgic
memory.

Then I remember, "Mares Eat Oats," "Chickery
Chick Cha La Cha La," or "The Little Man That Wasn't
There." ("Last night I saw upon the stair, The little
man who wasn't there. He wasn't there again today,
Oh how I wish he'd go away!") I realize our generation had its share of stupid songs. But they were our
stupid songs, and that made them special. I hear one

or two notes of a song of the 1940s and can sing all of the words immediately. It won't be too hard for the present generation to remember the words because some songs have only one phrase or one or two words. The beat is what is important, not the words.

I am more of a ballad person. I like the song to tell a story. The tears shed listening to "Honey" ("See the tree, how big it's grown...") would embarrass me if anyone saw me crying. But the song really moved me.

I remember songs that my older brothers and sisters sang before I became part of the Hit Parade Generation. One that sticks in my mind is "There ought to be a moonlight savings time, So I could love that gal of mine, And keep on loving overtime, 'til morning." I doubt that song will go down as a classic, but I think of it many a moonlight night. Others of that era were, "High upon a hilltop, beautiful to see, You and me together, underneath the trees." Or "Just Molly and me, and baby makes three, Are living in my blue heaven."

When my own children came along, I became immersed in different types of songs, "Jack was every inch a sailor," "The Teddy Bear's Picnic" and the long popular, "Davy Crockett" (Killed him a b'ar when he was only three!). As the kids grew older, I became used to, and even fond of, the Beach Boys, and finally the Beatles. But none of them became as much a part of me as those songs from the 1940s.

The war years made each song more meaningful. We can never forget the songs that reminded us of our beloved soldier far away. As much a part of me as the hymns we sing in church each Sunday are: "It's Been a Long, Long Time," "Saturday Night Is the Loneliest Night in the Week," "Waiting for the Train to Come in," "There'll Be Bluebirds over the White Cliffs of Dover," and the revival of World War I songs, "My Buddy," and "As Time Goes By."

I cherish distinct memories of lying in a darkened bedroom listening to my records (we had to get up and turn them over each time then). Many middle age plus persons share this memory. Let us join in singing, "It seems to me I've heard that song before."

MILLIONS OF RICHES

Everybody wants to be a millionaire these days. By marriage, by answering questions on a quiz show, or by surviving in deserted places, hundreds of people of all ages try their hand at becoming rich. Remember the $64,000 Question? We thought that was an unbelievable amount of money to win in a show. Now contestants sail past that figure early in the challenge. A million dollars isn't what it used to be. But then neither are some other prices and wages we deal with today.

When I was in college, I earned extra money by baby-sitting, often for the children of professors or university employees. I received twenty-five cents an hour. The rate was set by the university when they gave parents the list of approved sitters. Sometimes I came home around midnight with $1.50. Some of the parents objected to the price. Often they asked me if I would do it for less. After all, I could sit there and study while I was getting rich! I always replied that I would get in trouble with the university if I took less. I never wavered.

In the afternoons, I also worked in the Agriculture Economics office doing paper work that computers do in an instant today. I also received twenty-five cents an hour for that. After Lester and I were married, and he was discharged from the Army, I worked at the university library while he finished his degree on the G.I. Bill. I received $129.00 a month for a forty-hour week. I enjoyed this work in the catalog department and felt lucky to have the job because there were hundreds of G.I. wives trying to supplement their income while their husbands finished their degrees.

We were fortunate that we didn't have to pay rent, just utilities, since we were taking care of a family home while an estate was pending. We actually had more spending money that year than in many of the later years, even with that small salary.

Now that we have more expenses, I still won't attempt to make a million by being on the survivor shows. I would probably be the first one voted off and would have to live with that rejection the rest of my life.

I have quit sending in chances for sweepstakes but still receive messages saying I may be a winner. I used to have fun imagining what I would do if Ed McMann did appear at my door with the check. Now I prefer to imagine what I'll do with what I get the old fashioned way—by earning it.

It's easier now because one of the benefits of being middle age plus is that we need to get rid of things rather than acquire them. However, it would be fun to have a cook, a cleaning person, and maybe even a gardener. Actually some of those might be a possibility in the future. It won't be because I get rich but because I'd need Meals on Wheels, Living Assistance, or have to move where the employees of the facility care for the lawn.

I prefer my present lifestyle. I won't attempt to be a millionaire, but I will live like one in my own home, with my own things, and enjoy watching the wildlife around our Bronze Pond. It isn't golden, but it has lots of riches for us.

THE GIFT OF FRIENDSHIP

I don't know how anyone can live without friends and family. We have been so blessed with both that it is hard to visualize existence without this support.

For several weeks I drove daily to Joplin to spend the day with Lester when he was in the hospital. I took side streets to avoid the stop lights on Main Street. Early each morning, near the bus station, I noticed a woman pushing a cart filled with bulging garment bags. She wore an abundance of clothes, a big black hat, and very large shoes,

The first time I saw her, I thought she was going to take a bus. Each day I saw her again in the same neighborhood and decided that she must be a 'bag lady.'

My interest in her grew as I watched her each morning. Sometimes she was sitting on the sidewalk by the bus station. Other times she was crossing the street from the south. I asked one of our many minister friends who called on Lester about this woman and learned that she has regular routes she takes each day, and that she actually has money so that she could rent a room somewhere. She does not associate with the other homeless people but has her own solitary lifestyle which she repeats every day.

254 For Everything There Is a Season

Every time I passed, I wondered what I could do to help her but was told that she refuses help from agencies, churches, and individuals.

After arriving at the hospital and seeing the dozens of get-well cards adorning Lester's room and hearing about friends who called on him, I soon forgot my worries about the woman stranger. As we exchanged information from phone calls we each received, we frequently remarked how fortunate we were to know so many wonderful people in so many different places.

Our friends established new circles, so that one call to a certain person gave information about Lester's health to a whole congregation or neighborhood. As he recovered following surgery, we commented that his illness made us realize that each community where we had lived enriched us. And, from the outpouring of concern, perhaps we also did a little for them. In spite of all the anxiety and discomfort, there have been real gifts in this experience. (Of course, it's easy for me to say when I wasn't the one hurting—physically, at least.)

Retracing my route home at the end of the day took me back past the bus station. Never did I see the woman in the afternoons, only in the mornings. Filled with the support we received from our friends and family members as well as the kind people at the hospital, I again worried about this seemingly friendless woman.

What is her life story? Where is her family? Doesn't she have any friends? Why has she chosen this way of living when she has other choices?

The contrast between her life and ours was so marked during those days when our paths crossed briefly that I almost felt guilty. I don't know that I can change her life in any way, but perhaps I can befriend another person somewhere who feels unloved. It may be too late for anything but professional help for this lady, but a smile or encouraging word can't do any harm.

In the meantime, I will try to express our thanks and appreciation for all everyone did for us during Lester's illness and always be grateful that wherever I might be in Missouri and many other states, it wouldn't take me long to find a friend.

For that, I am constantly thankful.

DRY SOCKS, CLEAN SHEETS AND THE FEEL OF A WARM HAND

As I get older I find I get comfort from a lot of little things that I never thought much about before. For instance, there is the pleasure of putting on a clean, dry pair of socks.

I do lawn mowing on our lawn tractor and wear sturdy shoes and socks to protect my feet from chiggers and from anything flying from the blades of the mower. In hot weather my feet get quite warm and sweaty inside all that protection. As soon as I finish the job, I take off my shoes and socks. Then after a bath to hopefully wash off any little chiggers hanging around, I put on clean, dry socks. It feels really comforting to my feet.

When we go on canoe float trips on the river, we wear canvas shoes so that when we get in and out of the canoe, or when we have to pull the canoe over low places, we can walk without puncturing our feet on the Ozark rocks in the river bed. After a day of floating, swimming (still with shoes on), and visiting the gravel bars for lunch, our feet feel puckered and raw.

A dry pair of shoes and socks waiting at the end of the day feels heavenly. Unless there are many other hale and hearty persons to take care of all the coolers, life preservers, and towels from the day's trip, there is no way we can go barefoot on the gravel bars where we take out. Doing these clean-up jobs in dry shoes, especially with dry socks inside, is much easier.

Flannel pajamas on a cool night also brings a luxurious sense of comfort, especially if they haven't shrunk up in the dryer and still fit nicely.

Sitting in the shade of a tree on the lawn when there is a nice breeze and enjoying a cool drink can make any day's hard work seem more than worthwhile. Sharing this moment with another person, a pet, or even a good book, gives still more rewards.

Good music, birds singing, sunsets, sunrises, and moonlight nights all bring much joy to me, but none of them can compare to the joy of getting into bed with fresh, clean sheets. When I was small, we never had both sheets brand clean at the same time. Every week my mother moved the top sheet to the bottom when she put the bottom sheet in the laundry. We enjoyed a clean top sheet, but a slightly used bottom one. This was a practical solution for a family with ten people sleeping in at least five beds. The only time I experienced two clean sheets at once was in a hotel on our trips.

Recently in a hotel where I stayed for several days, there was a little sign requesting us to let the management know if we did not need clean sheets each day. They promised they would make up the bed and bring clean towels, but using the same sheets over again, would help the environment tremendously. I read the notice and agreed, but my, it was tempting to indulge in daily clean sheets. Since I had a king-sized bed, and Lester wasn't with me, I moved to the other side of the bed the second night to get some of the clean-sheet feeling. The next morning after I got home, I changed our sheets to prolong the luxury.

Probably the best feeling I experience in these later years is the feel of a hand in mine. Sometimes it is a little hand that reaches for mine as we walk together. Other times it is an even smaller hand encircling one of my fingers as generations get acquainted. Occasionally it is a helping hand to give me a boost up when I am carrying a load. But most often the pleasure comes from another hand that is also covered with aging spots and some wrinkles as we share a moment together.

It is even more meaningful if we both have on clean dry socks!

PIECES OF THE PUZZLE

I have been working jigsaw puzzles lately. I once set up one that had a thousand pieces. That was a mistake. It took forever for all of us to put it together.

While our Texas family was visiting us after Christmas, Joan helped set up another puzzle of five hundred pieces. Though that one went more quickly, it still took a long time.

The trouble with me and jigsaw puzzles is that I don't know when to stop. I think I will sit down for a few minutes to put a few pieces in before continuing with my work. But after I find a place for one piece, or two or three, I am encouraged to look for that funny little corner piece, or one with just a splash of red on one side. Hours go by instead of the planned few minutes.

I get such a feeling of accomplishment when I find each piece. A completed puzzle becomes a treasure I save. What a disappointment we had when we couldn't complete the large thousand-piece puzzle because there was one piece missing! We searched the floor and chairs in vain for the elusive piece. The masterpiece remained incomplete.

We middle age plus people are a little like that thousand-piece puzzle. Myriads of little pieces fitted together have made our lives as they are today. We have bright pieces with distinctive shapes that are easy to identify as special times—a wedding, birth of a child, finishing a project, or feeling good about something we have done. Those pieces fit in easily and are fun to work with.

But there are all those small similar pieces of dark and drab colors that fill in the background. It takes several inches to form a frame that holds together the colorful, exciting shapes. Fitting these together is not nearly as much fun, nor is it as colorful, but the puzzle has no real picture without these essential but uninteresting pieces. Likewise, the day-by-day pieces of the majority of our lives don't stand out for any particular reason but fit together with another small drab piece to support the really special days.

Most of us in the older generation have not yet completed our life puzzles. That one piece, or a hundred pieces, are still missing. We can't see the total picture because there are always more pieces to fit into those blank spots. Looking under the table or chairs will not find the pieces because they are not really missing. They haven't been formed yet.

Even though the picture shows much promise, and we see how we think it is going to look, we can't be sure because those missing pieces can alter the entire life puzzle with a surprise. Nor can we look at the picture on the box to see what it should look like. We have to wait to discover the shape of the piece and where it will fit.

While I hate to find a piece missing from my boxed jigsaws, I am excited to know that in my life puzzle

there is still room for many more pieces. Later someone else will have to view the completed picture to
decide if it is a treasure or rather drab and uninteresting.

Section Eight

A TIME TO DANCE

Now is the time to join the dance
To celebrate the season.
And if it's not some special day
Then dance for any reason!

MODERN FAMILIES MAKE THANKSGIVING DIFFICULT

It will soon be time to go over the river and through the woods to Grandmother's house for Thanksgiving. But which Grandmother? When the song was written not too many families were blessed with even two grandmothers who lived within a reasonable horse-and-buggy ride. Now with people, especially women, living longer, some families have so many grandmothers that they couldn't possibly go to all of them in any given holiday. On top of that, we would have to reach many grandmothers by over the highways and into the sky to Grandmother's house we fly.

I have always tried to cooperate with my co-grandparents and share these special days by having our gathering at a time other than the traditional noon on Thursday. This year I am getting a jump start on all of them by having a Thanksgiving Eve celebration. That way I will be the first one that the kids, grandkids, and great grandkids visit. (I started to put in the words "have to" but decided that wasn't in the holiday spirit.)

Mine will be the first turkey, the first cranberry sauce, the first sweet potatoes, and the first pumpkin pie. They won't be comparing what they eat here with an identical meal they ate at the other Grandma's house that noon or the day before.

This hasn't happened to me very often. I have had our gathering on the Saturday or Sunday after the official day more often than this early date. By then the little kids are so stressed out that they are either little walking zombies, or are so hyped up from all the sweets and attention that they can't sit still. But this time they will be eager to see everyone, be looking forward to the big meal and will remember the occasion fondly. Oh well, I can dream, can't I?

I haven't checked the football schedule yet. If the Kansas City Chiefs or the University of Missouri are not playing on Wednesday night then perhaps we can even eat without the television on. Since our two Texas families will not be making the trip north this year, we will have only our Missouri contingent. That means there will be only fourteen here unless my sister and niece accept my invitation. That doesn't seem quite right. We usually have over twenty, but we will have a little more elbow room this year.

The children of our grandson, Michael, and his wife, Carrie, Shelbie, Jordan, and Jerron, have grandmothers they don't even know—great-great-grandmother on Michael's side as well as two great-grandmothers (I am one), a grandmother, and step-grandmother, etcetera, etcetera, etcetera.

Some are too far away to consider visiting for the holiday, but since most of them are within a two or three county area, the poor children get hugged and kissed so often they feel like celebrities. After about two days of this, they begin to show that they are only very tired children.

As our group is smaller this year, and I will be starting off the season for our loved ones, I am going to do more from-scratch cooking. I will actually pour the canned filling into the frozen crusts instead of buying the pies from Koehn's. I will put the stove-top stuffing into my turkey instead of just having a separate dish. And I will put brown sugar over the frozen sweet potato patties before I warm them up. Nothing is too good for this special day.

I intend to make my special salad which no one likes except the Texas families who won't be here, and I will cook whole cranberries if I remember to buy some to supplement the canned cranberry sauce.

On Wednesday night when many of you will still be baking and planning your big event, you can think of us already sitting down with our family to a typical Thornton celebration. Will you share with me my pleasure in being the first this year?

I just got a phone call from my son. His mother-in-law is having his family over the Sunday before instead of on Thanksgiving day this year. I hope her turkey is all stringy and dry!

OOPS!

I once baked two turkeys for the Soroptomist Annual Turkey Dinner. Cooking a turkey used to be a frightening thing to do with numerous peeks into the oven to test whether the bird was done or not and constant basting to keep the big fellow from drying out while he was roasting. I always had trouble getting the feet untied or unfastened from the metal clips attached to the legs. If the turkey wasn't well defrosted (I wonder, does anyone start with a bird that has not been frozen anymore?), then I had trouble getting the neck out of the body cavity and the rest of the little organs from the sack in his neck.

Now I have learned to defrost the bird slowly for several days and plop him into a turkey roasting sack. When the proper time has elapsed, I check to see if the little red button has popped out and remove the bird. I have a clean oven, a nice moist bird, and a relatively clean roasting pan. That is, all that is possible if you have mastered the next step, which I have not.

This step is getting the bird out of the roasting sack, keeping the drippings for the gravy, and preserving the bird in one glorious piece for carving while it is at least still slightly warm. When I try to raise the bird out of its cozy sack, the tender meat immediately falls off the bones, the drippings live up to their name on my hands, and I trail turkey juice and bits of meat all over the stove. The visions of an attractive platter with a few sprigs of greenery around it disappear as I struggle to keep the fowl intact.

This was not a problem at the Soroptomist dinner for we were instructed to bring the turkey already sliced and placed in pans for additional warming. No one had to know all that I went through before getting the pieces in the pan. But I will say that at no time did the bird, or any part of it, hit the floor, and our cats greatly enjoyed all the scrap pieces I kept creating.

For the family Thanksgiving, I'd like to serve an attractive-looking platter with a nice golden bird placed neatly in the middle. I probably won't. I probably will bake the bird the day before, cut him up, and serve the pieces from my attractive platter. The family really doesn't care, and by now they are used to my flops as a cook. But I do think it would be nice once in a while to have a Norman-Rockwell-type setting.

Then I realize that two grandsons will probably eat with their caps on backwards throughout the meal, the great-granddaughters will want to sit by me in the one high chair we have, and the adults will want to watch the football game on television. Maybe it doesn't matter at all what the food looked like.

I wonder what would happen if I just ordered in a pizza!

ALL I WANT FOR CHRISTMAS IS TO BE IMPARTIAL

I just got a catalog to select last minute gifts for Christmas. I don't consider early December as last minute. Christmas Eve is last minute. Maybe even December 23rd is getting close. But at the first of December there is lots of time.

Have you noticed that often when you greet people in December the question isn't, "How are you?" Instead it is, "Have you finished your Christmas shopping yet?" This is usually answered with a groan and eye-rolling to imply that not only are you not finished, but you doubt that you ever will be.

That is one reason I don't shop early. If I do, then I will invariably run into two or three more things that would be just perfect for the person I already finished shopping for. If I succumb to the temptation to get the additional items, I have to run down all my list and add extras to other people's gifts because I don't want to be unfair.

I love shopping for teenagers. All they want is money. I can buy it with one check at the bank. Since I want to dress it up a bit and make it seem more like a gift, I buy a little token figurine or toy to go along with the green stuff. Then realizing that made the value of the gift more than the cosmetic case I gave his cousin, I get a little something extra for her as well. If I wait till the last minute, I don't have time for all those second thoughts and added extras. I must be efficient and go down my list systematically to cross off each relative as I make a purchase.

My childhood Christmas shopping in Washington, D.C. was much simpler. Our mother took my sister Ellen and me to the big dime store downtown and gave each of us one dollar to buy presents for our seven siblings and our parents. She stood at the door to wait for us as we shopped. Sometimes we went together until we had to separate to select the gifts for each other. If I had any money left over I would get a handkerchief for my teacher. If not then my mother would give us an extra dime to make that last purchase.

I wonder what on earth grade school teachers did with all those handkerchiefs. At that time people actually did use cloth hankies for blow as well as show. But yearly each teacher got more than a dozen. Probably some teachers' children are still pondering this question as they hate to dispose of the drawer full of lacy handkerchiefs which their mother carefully saved and never used.

Wrapping the presents was something special. We tried to be creative or funny, such as wrapping a small item inside a series of boxes to make it look big. By the time all eight of us put our gifts under the tree in the living room, the pile of gifts filled a corner of the room. Yet we didn't spend many dollars in total.

We all tend to get nostalgic this time of year and wish for the old days when things were simpler. But some of my modern gifts have really been meaningful to me. I would never have baked any home made bread if my daughter-in-law hadn't given me a bread machine. I would have hacked the poor turkey to pieces if my son hadn't given me the electric knife a few years ago. Sweat shirts, flannel pajamas, pictures of the children, and books have all been treasured gifts through the years.

One Christmas Lester and the children went together to give me a set of dining room chairs to match our table. Susan and Lester carefully arranged them around the table on Christmas morning. I rushed through the dining room to get breakfast, went back again twice, and finally had to be told to look at the table.

That was a far cry from the little girl that used to look in every closet and drawer to try to find gifts before the big day. When you are middle age plus I guess you have other things on your mind. Such as, "Did I give Chris more than I gave Les?"

CHRISTMAS MUSIC

Christmas music is one of the best things about the season. My grown children laughed at my habit of having Christmas records playing most of the time between Thanksgiving and Christmas. I don't do that any more. I play CDs instead! Or I listen to public radio for classical Christmas music.

My routine of playing all my favorites while I am trimming the house puts me in the mood for all the rest of the season. I started to say OLD favorites, but then I realized that some of the special songs I enjoy are relatively new.

When I was in college, I bought an album of Judy Garland's Christmas favorites. In it she sang "Star of the East." I had not heard this song before, and at first I was disappointed that her album didn't contain more of the church-type carols. But now this song has become very special to me.

A song that was introduced to our family in the 1960s is "The Little Drummer Boy." Our youngest son's chorus sang this in the school assembly with Mark carrying the part of the drumming notes. Our neighbor was so impressed by his rendition that she gave us a Christmas centerpiece featuring the little drummer boy. When I placed this ornament while playing the song again, I was warmed by thought of both Mark and Louise.

I didn't like the Advent songs in church years ago. I was impatient for the minister to start using 'real' Christmas songs. As we became more involved in understanding the season of Advent when Lester became a minister, I found a new favorite in "O Come, O Come, Immanuel." I'll have to admit that one of the reasons I like it so well is that it is quite low, in a minor key. I can sing it without having all the children in church turn around to look at me because of my low voice. Another of my favorites that I can't sing at all, because it is too high, is "Angels We Have Heard on High." I can still listen to it and enjoy hearing others sing it.

Funny Christmas songs also have a place in my heart. When "All I Want for Christmas Is My Two Front Teeth" first became popular, my mother was having her teeth pulled to get her first dentures. She was unhappy about having no teeth for a week or two during the healing process. It happened that it came at Christmas time. So I presented her with the sheet music for that song. As she read the words to us at the Christmas table amid much laughter, she relaxed about her toothless smile. I laughed with her, in memory, again this year when I heard the song. Thankfully, with improved dental care, I haven't faced that toothless phase. Perhaps my dentist has become carried away with another song he sings in our choir, "Crown Him with Many Crowns," because I boast quite a few crowns over my 'real' teeth.

While I was listening to one of Bing Crosby's Christmas songs on a good quality disc, I was thankful for these inventions that let us hear this singer many years after his death. I thought how great it would be to have that possibility with the voices of my parents.

Christmas songs played on the flute remind me of our youngest daughter. Another daughter's clarinet tunes stir other memories. And the angel Gabriel's trumpet will not drown out thoughts of our oldest son's music. Though none of them use these instruments now, each Christmas program I see reawakens the feeling of watching our own children proclaim the Christmas message through music.

Now we have a fourth generation in school, which brings another round of Christmas programs and songs to enjoy again through these young ones.

I may not have my Christmas shopping done yet, but I sure have a good start on my Christmas memories. I just hope that I am also creating some memories for others to recall when I'm past middle age plus!

SANTA CLAUS COMES TONIGHT

I was late putting up my Christmas tree this year. I do not like to put up the tree when I am in a hurry because I have a little ritual I carry out while doing my decorating.

I like to take each ornament and remember where we got it, who made it for us, and how many different homes this ornament has brightened.

When we were first married, we had only a tree and maybe a display of our Christmas cards. Each year I add more until now we have decorations for every room and almost every corner of every room. These decorations are not the stylish, color coordinated ones seen in magazine illustrations. Some of them are rather seedy looking, but they add a special meaning to our Christmases.

For example, we have a light bulb our son, Mark, made into a Santa head when he was in Cub Scouts. He now has sons of his own who are too old for Cub Scouts, but we still hang this Santa on the tree with his straggly beard and faded felt hat. Our granddaughter, Penny, made an angel for the top of our tree several years ago. Since it gets smashed easily when I pack it away, it has lost some of its personality. I still put this angel out each year, not always on the top of the tree, but somewhere. A box of gold ornaments take me back to our first Christmas together (and my first away from my own family) when these were the only ornaments I had for a cedar tree cut from my mother-in-law's pasture.

Dated decorations from Hallmark remind me of friends in Independence who worked there and shared some of the bounty given to employees. Beautifully crafted ornaments made by various church members in churches Lester served bring back memories of dear friends, many of whom are no longer alive.

Large Christmas balls decorated with the names of each of our four children remind me of my sister Miriam who gave a ball for each child's first Christmas.

Secret sister gifts from club, ornaments bought at our own recent church bazaar, Christmas card holders from childhood friends, and discount store trinkets bought while shopping with a good friend have all added to the meaning of our decorations. To complete the emotion of the occasion, I try to sing or listen to Christmas songs while assembling the decorations. I always start with the song my mother sang to us each Christmas Eve as we were going to bed. "Hang your stocking in a row, Santa Claus comes tonight."

Even when we are middle age plus we are still kids at Christmas time.

IT'S SNOW FUN

Are you ready to play in the snow? Some of my favorite memories involve different ways to enjoy snow.

When I was young, I was an avid sledder. Near our home in Washington, D.C. was a park that was the remains of a Revolutionary War fort. The bulwarks on top of a natural hill made a wonderful spot for sledding.

We belly-flopped on the sled at the top of the embankment, glided down the hill, across a level area, down a steep terrace to the street where we continued our ride for another block or more. This street was often closed during snowy weather.

When there were more children than sleds, we rode double-up or even triple-up, all lying on our tummies. Holding the sled in front of him, the first child ran and flopped down on the sled. The second ran alongside and piled on top a little farther on to avoid slowing down the sled. The third, and this was often my spot because I was the smallest, frantically jumped on top of the other two bodies for the long ride.

The heavier the sled's load, the faster it went. But also, the higher the pile of young bodies, the more chances for spills. I had my share of spills from the top of this racing tower of children. I guess I was considered a cry baby when I was little because I was always trying to keep up with older kids. I didn't cry, though, when sledding for fear my tears would freeze on my face.

In the places we lived in Missouri it was too flat for me to enjoy sledding with our own children. We shared other winter fun. All ages have enjoyed ice skating, or just slipping and sliding on our frozen farm pond the few times it has been cold enough, long enough to make certain the ice was safe.

I never enjoyed a snowball fight, but I do love to make snow people, snow forts for others to fight behind, and other sculptures out of snow.

My favorite snow game is fox and geese. I played that as a child and with my children. If it snows when my grandchildren visit, I'll play it with them. This game consists of running like crazy in circled paths formed in the snow while trying to elude the chasing fox. If the fox catches all the geese, then the first one caught becomes the fox and the running begins again. Part of the fun of the game is joining together to tramp out the playing field to begin the game. The beautiful smooth snow soon becomes a race track for young energy.

Running this hard in bitter cold weather caused pain in our lungs as we gasped for breath. But we never admitted we needed to slow down. One of the good things about this sport is that all we need is snow, space, and people. No batteries are required.

When the game gets old, we rest by falling backward in the unspoiled snow to make beautiful snow angels.

I have to admit that now some of my enjoyment

of snow comes from quiet walks in the frozen beauty
or even gazing out the windows from a warm room.

WHAT ARE YOU DOING
NEW YEAR'S EVE?

New Year's Eve has special meaning. It is a time to finish up the old year and get a fresh start. For many it is a time to have fun and attend parties. Others like to spend it in a religious Watch Party at a church. Many Middle Age Plus people treat it like any other night, go to bed at the usual time and wake early to watch the Rose Bowl Parade.

My memories of special New Year's Eve begin in high school. A girlfriend and I gave a New Year's Eve party in her house. We had several girls to invite, but we had problems thinking up enough boys that we thought would possibly come. I got up my nerve and invited Fremont Hobson who sat behind me in home room. His father had some important government job, but growing up in Washington, D.C., we were used to having friends whose fathers (then it was never the mothers) were important figures in government. It didn't seem to make any difference in the way the student was viewed by the rest of us in the school. The father of one of the most popular girls was a policeman in the neighborhood.

Back to Fremont. We were too young to drive. Fremont's father picked me up and drove us the mile to my girlfriend's house. The party was not a howling success. Betty's mother tried to liven it up by having a conga line going around the living room, dining room, and kitchen, and then back to the living room. I remember having trouble remembering to kick at the right time. Mr. Hobson took us home soon after midnight. In my yearbook Fremont wrote, "I will always remember New Year's Eve of 1942." I wasn't sure if he remembered it because it was so awful for him, or if he enjoyed it. I think it was the former because he never asked me for a date after that.

The next year another boy took me to a hotel ballroom for a New Year's Eve celebration. We had to take the street car to get there because of gas restrictions during the war. Our cokes cost a tremendous amount but the band was good, and we moved around a little on the small dance floor. It was too crowded to really dance, and we weren't that good at it anyway. This was the first time I experienced the lighting effect of colored lights focused on a revolving ball of shaped glass. Now we see it in every skating rink. Then it was breath-taking.

A really memorable New Year's Eve happened when my sister and I came to Columbia to attend the University of Missouri. We drove through snow to have time before classes began to reach Nevada for a New Year's Eve square dance. It was held on the second floor of a building east on Highway 54. It was what we then called a road house. However, this was a private neighborhood party. Don and Richard Johnson played for it along with some other local musicians. Like the postal service, neither snow, sleet, nor hail could keep us from getting back for this party.

Many years later I remember another special New Year's Eve when the weather was bad. Everyone was snowed in and getting cabin fever. Verner Franks pulled into our driveway with a tractor pulling a wagon loaded with several other neighboring families seated in the hay. He said, "Bundle up the kids, grab whatever you have to eat, and come with us to our house." We followed his directions and joined the Tyers, Gasts, and others on the wagon for a marvelous evening at the Franks' home. We played pitch while the kids played with each other and eventually filled all of Mildred's beds as they fell asleep. We enjoyed the varied refreshments and were delivered home about one o'clock.

Another card party on New Year's Eve sticks in my mind when we were in north Missouri, and had invited another family to join us for the evening. It began snowing while we played cards and it didn't stop until we had eighteen or nineteen inches. The young ones ran out in the snow to bang on pans at midnight.

However you celebrate this New Year's Eve, I am sure you will be like me in remembering those friends and loved ones that shared earlier years with you. Happy New Year!

BE MY VALENTINE

Pleasant and not so pleasant memories of Valentine's Day are plentiful. As I get older, it no longer hurts that Freddie Bates didn't give me a valentine in the fifth grade. I can laugh now when I picture him in his corduroy knickers and button-down-the-front sweater to think that I ever cared whether he put a valentine for me in the big crepe paper-covered box at the front of the classroom. He probably didn't put one in for any of the girls. I was afraid to ask the others, but since he sat right behind me, I thought he'd at least give me one. He didn't. It is odd that even though it wasn't a dig deal, I remember this sixty years later.

Small hurts of childhood can blow over quickly, or they can remain fixed in our minds forever. What makes it hard for parents, grandparents, and great-grandparents is not knowing which act of omission or word carelessly spoken will be the one that stays fixed in the child's memory. That worry is partly what prompts us grandparents to 'spoil' our grandkids.

Today, children receive not only the traditional paper valentine cards, but in many schools during the day, they receive flowers or 'message balloons.' Pity the poor child or youth who leaves school on February the fourteenth without a balloon bobbing overhead. Parents sometimes send these greetings to their child to be sure there is at least one remembrance to carry home. Although there is certainly nothing wrong with a parent expressing love on this day, I am sure that most youngsters would prefer that their balloons came from someone their own age, preferably one of the opposite sex.

I am trying to clear out some of the accumulation of papers, letters, and printed materials from the years so someone else won't have the task later. When I come to the crayon-colored valentines from my children or grandchildren, I put them right back in the drawer. Someone else will have to throw them out. I can't. Maybe those who sent them years ago will enjoy seeing them again and will keep them among their treasures. I won't be the one that destroyed the greeting.

Of all the valentines I have ever received, the one most treasured was when our daughter, Shirley, gave birth to Kevin, our third grandchild. Even though this gift of a baby wasn't expressly for me but was shared by two families, it is one that I will always cherish. And he continues to improve with age.

MARCH WINDS BRING...

In Missouri late winter/early springtime weather can be quite different from one day to the next. I am hoping that March first will be cold and stormy. That's an odd thing to wish for, but I want March to come in like a lion so it will go out like a lamb.

The late 1950s and early 60s we had some very cold weather in March. One time we had the biggest snowfalls of the year in the middle of March. Our collie dog had a litter of seven very small pups. We kept them in an old brooder house to keep warm but Topsy wanted to be out with us. It seemed like all I did that month was clean the floor after tracking snow and mud from the frequent trips to oversee the pups.

Another March memory was more painful. Lester had spotted some redbud trees when they were blooming the year before. Knowing that I love redbud trees, he took the whole family to the spot where we dug up some little trees to plant in our lawn. The trees did fine and flourished, but they evidently had some undesirable close neighbors because I got the worst case of poison ivy of my adult life. There was no foliage on any trees or bushes, but that didn't keep the venom from some ivy plant giving me a painful remembrance of an otherwise pleasant day.

During my school years in Washington, D.C., March was always the signal to do two things. First we would get some strong paper and thin sticks and make a kite which we decorated gaily. I don't remember ever really flying any of those we made because they invariably were not strong enough to do the job. So our second ritual was to go to the little neighborhood store at the corner of Fessenden Street and Wisconsin Avenue to buy a commercial kite kit. We didn't get the kites already put together. Our purchase consisted of two thin lathes of wood with notched ends and a strong, diamond-shaped paper with short sections of string fixed in each corner of the diamond to hook onto the notches in the wood lathes. Usually some string came with the kite, but we always got some extra so that we could fly our kite higher than the other kids who gathered at the nearby park on the site of historic Fort Bayer.

Our own kids had some kites similar to those I remember from my youth, but our grandkids and great-grandkids all have sturdy plastic kites made in various shapes and colors. I don't suppose they have any more fun with them than we did with ours years ago.

March was also a time when we began roller skating to school again after the snowy weather was over. A well-dressed school child wore a skate key on a string around her neck so that she could fasten the clamp-on skates tightly to her sturdy oxfords. Our skates were designed to adjust in length so we could use the same skates for several years if we took good care of them. Teachers often warned us against jumping the curbs to skate across intersections, but it didn't do much more good than telling the same thing to the skateboarders of today. We were lucky to live in a neighborhood with very little traffic and several wonderfully long blocks.

In my present state, my expectations of March are much milder. I look forward to seeing our returning Canada geese making another nest on our pond and seeing the first crocus blooms under our oak trees. I begin thinking that since I didn't do any deep fall housecleaning, maybe I should think about doing it this spring.

I don't need to start that yet because March probably still has some wintry surprises in store for us. I don't want to get too involved in window washing and all that good stuff until I am sure it will stay warm.

If you think I am just using the weather as an excuse for being lazy and not wanting to clean house, then I'll tell you to go fly a kite!

WHITE HOUSE
EGG-ROLLING—1930s

I heard a health professional on television state that if a hard-boiled Easter egg has been out of refrigeration for more than four hours, it should be thrown away. When I heard that, I had to pinch myself to be sure that I was still alive. With that warning, I should not have survived past ten years of age.

In my childhood we boiled and colored eggs on Saturday, kept them in our Easter baskets along with candy and little toy chicks and ducks through Easter Sunday. Then on Easter Monday we had an egg-rolling. After the eggs cracked sufficiently from rolling down hill on the ground, we ate them. Sometimes we competed to see who could eat the most eggs on that day.

In Washington, D.C., we often took part in the Easter Egg-Rolling on the White House lawn. Our mother liked to go to hear the band and be part of the excitement. We liked to go so we could finally eat our eggs. Before we rolled our eggs, Mrs. Roosevelt made an address, which we children didn't listen to. There were facilities to get water and eat our picnic lunch wherever our group wanted.

What I remember most clearly were the toilets. In those days there was no Porta Potty company to supply this need. There was a long narrow tent with wooden benches equipped with appropriate holes along the bench. I assume there was something underneath to catch our deposits, but I wasn't concerned about that then. I was impressed with the community atmosphere of sitting side by side with a dozen or so women and girls, all with the same purpose in mind. (When the Ringling Bros. Circus came to town there was a similar arrangement for their patrons.)

Now that I am middle age plus and have been responsible for supplying facilities for family gatherings and church events, I wish I had paid more attention to the mechanics of this makeshift arrangement.

I don't remember that the White House lawn was defaced in any way by this setup, but I do remember leaving the grounds and seeing trash, cracked eggshells, and broken Easter baskets strewn all over the lawn.

Even though my main memories are more earthy than historical, I am still glad that my mother allowed my sister and me to partake of an event that is unique to our country. I hope the children that gather at the White House each Easter Monday will know that they shouldn't eat those eggs if they have been out of the refrigerator for four hours. It would be awful if they grew up to be like I am because I ate eggs that had been cooked at least forty-eight hours earlier!

MAY DAY FUN

The early part of May brings back good memories—celebrations of May Day when we were children. Recently I visited a woman my age who had never been involved in wrapping a May Pole. Since this was a yearly tradition in my childhood, I was surprised to learn that everyone hadn't shared this fun/confusion/madhouse routine sometime in childhood.

The kindergarten children in my school did the Maypole dance each year for their parents. Usually one child going the wrong way got the intricate weaving of the colored strands haplessly tangled. But the mothers clapped dutifully anyway.

One time a neighbor tried to have a party for the children on May Day. She erected a pole, getting long strands of ribbons and showing all of the kids how to make a beautifully wrapped pole. She didn't take into account that her own son was not the cooperative type. He began tying up the little girls with the ribbons strands. The party disintegrated quickly.

A more successful part of our May Day celebration was fixing little homemade paper baskets and filling them with flowers. We'd take them to neighbors' homes, ring the bell, and run away. These neighbor women opened the door to see the little flower offerings on their doorstep while we watched from the bushes. They exclaimed loudly (for our benefit), "Well, look what's here! Where on earth did these beautiful flowers come from?"

It took all of our youthful self control to keep from revealing our hiding place and claiming ownership. We never dreamed our friends knew exactly who brought the bouquets.

During my junior high and high school years, our schools put on massive physical competition with other schools in events such as races, jumping, and other track skills. During the years, these May Day events took on more of a mass, organized display. I was in one such celebration that had over a hundred girls jumping rope in a choreographed sequence to the tune of "Pop Goes the Weasel." The entire field was filled with girls in gym suits lined up in rows of eight doing the same routine that two leaders on a high stage were performing.

This type of demonstration lost favor quickly when our relations with the U.S.S.R. deteriorated because it looked too much like the Communist May Day celebrations. It's really too bad. I still can't hear "Pop Goes the Weasel" without wanting to start jumping.

IN THE GOOD OLD SUMMERTIME

If I asked you to quickly share a happy childhood memory with me, what would it be? I would guess that your memory would be a summertime happening. Summertime and children seem to go together. The three month vacation from school stretched into endless days playing in the shade of a tree or nights lying on the grass looking up at the stars.

I don't ever remember being bored in the summer. Of course, in a big family we all had lots of chores to do that filled part of the day. But there were still uninterrupted hours for creative play.

My sister, our friend, Joyce, and I used to make endless playhouses out under the mulberry trees. We would scrounge some old kitchen utensils that my mother no longer used and set up our 'home' to begin cooking a meal. By crossing the fence into the corn field we could make a sumptuous meal from one puny ear of corn. (We knew better than to break off a good ear.) The corn silks made magnificent spaghetti or noodles, the husks served as our serving dishes, the grains of corn became whatever entrée we wanted to imagine, and the cobs broken into two candlesticks made our serving table more elegant.

Another time we might make this playhouse in an unused farm building where we were oblivious to the heat and bugs as we swept out debris and arranged 'furniture' to meet the needs of our pretend family. On rainy days we moved inside to lay playing cards on the floor to make outlines of a house. After designing the house, we cut out furniture from the catalog that hadn't made its way yet to the outhouse, and last, populated the house either with paper dolls or from the models from the same catalog. Most of the action within this designed house followed a plot that we made up as we played. Our children were always the brightest ones in the family and solved many intricate mysteries and problems.

The big elm trees in the front yard created opportunities for more active play. We always had one trapeze and a one rope swing that had a stick tied near the end of the rope for a child (or adult) to sit straddling the rope. While holding the rope she could push herself with her feet or beg a push from a sibling. We devised a way to propel ourselves by swinging into the sturdy trunk of the tree and pushing against it with our feet which would send us in ever increasing circles away from the tree, coming back for another push at the end of each circle. Other times we would climb, by ladder, up into a nearby elm tree carrying the end of the one rope swing, and swing off from the fork of that tree out past the big elm.

The trapeze offered other challenges such as hanging by our knees, or by our ankles, and even trying to chin ourselves. I never was good at that, but I could hang by my knees while swinging.

On days when we had no playmate, or when our energy level was not as high, we read and reread books from the family library, played familiar pieces on the piano, or wrote letters back to our friends in Washington, D.C. to tell them about our fun.

From the age of eleven on, I had the privilege of turning the family car around when someone returned from town and left the car at the lawn gate. My job was to drive the car down around the well curb and circle back to have it ready for the next trip off the farm. This was a ritual for the beginning driver to test skills before taking to the open road.

Of course there are also memories of hours standing by an ironing board in a hot kitchen while the irons heated on the stove waiting for the next change. My job was to iron my sister's and my cotton bloomers. Now I wonder why my mother insisted that they be ironed, but they always were. Another hot job was washing the dishes in the kitchen while one burner on the Perfection kerosene range kept the rinse water hot enough to scald the dishes in the rack.

When I am remembering my summer days, these work memories are crowded out by the visions of games of hide and seek, "Mother, May I?" and other fun times shared with friends and relatives under the trees.

No television, not even good radio, no computer or video games, no summer camp, no VCR movies, but we had fun, and we were never bored. We certainly knew better than to tell our parents we had nothing to do!

Section Nine

A TIME TO HEAL

A scar will show the hurt was there.
A kiss will let me know you care.

TWO EXPERIENCES

One nice thing about writing is that no matter what bad thing happens to me, I can feel better about it because I can have a new subject. The same thing goes for good things that happen. I can enjoy them even more because I can share them and experience double joy. I've had several experiences of each kind recently, but I will use only two, one mildly bad, and one good.

Let's start with the bad. There is a brand of salad dressing made in Carthage that my children really like which can't be bought in Texas. I usually give my Austin, Texas, daughter one or two bottles of it for gifts when she is home. Susan, in turn, has shared some of these gifts with others in her office and among her friends. To get some brownie points in her office, she asked me to send her several more bottles. I chose to buy them in cases, thinking they would be easier to mail in their shipping packages.

After picking up the two cases at the grocery store, I went to the post office and carried both cases in at one time, one on top of the other. That was a mistake. I should have taken two trips to the car, taking them one at a time. After friendly patrons of the post office helped me through both sets of doors which open toward the incoming, package-laden customer, I reached the counter intact.

Have you ever noticed how high the counters in the post office are if you have to lift a package up onto them? I tried to lift the two cases up together. I just couldn't do it. So I gracefully held the bottom case against the counter with my thighs while I lifted the top case onto the counter. Or at least that was my plan. It didn't work. When I lifted the top case off, something in the balance I had maintained while holding the load shifted, causing the bottom case to slide to the floor. I dropped the top case and then completely lost it, falling backward flat on my back on the lobby floor.

I looked up into the startled faces of several other customers and the clerk who had instantly come from behind the counter to help me up. He must have set a speed record because I popped up as quickly as I dropped down because I didn't want anyone to see what I had done. I could have two broken legs and still my pride would make me get up immediately. But since it was cold weather, I had on a thick coat and had built-in padding in most of the places where I landed. I was not really hurt, except my pride. As the boxes of dressing seemed okay. I mailed them on and have heard that they arrived in good shape with no leakage.

Now I am on a crusade to have post offices arrange their counters as the airlines do, with a low place handy for heavy packages to slide through to the clerk instead of lifting them to chest height. It would have saved me a tender wrist, and certainly kept the clerk from a near heart attack when he saw me take my fall.

Later in the week I attended a large meeting of United Methodist Women in Jefferson City. The keynote speaker, a long-time friend who has worked with me in many meeting, knowing what I do best, has called on me for assistance several times during her presentations. Shortly before she was introduced, she asked me and two other women to help her at a certain point in her talk. She wanted us to lead the singing of a song that carried out her theme, "I Want to Teach The World To Sing in Perfect Harmony."

I protested that she should chose some one else for she knew I wasn't a good singer. She answered, "Carolyn that's why I chose you." Knowing I didn't sing well, she wanted our trio to sound awful, so she could stop us and make a point about harmony. Then the whole group would sing the song melodiously.

I was exalted. For years I have been isolated by my bad singing voice. I even had one choir director ask me not to sing so loud in the congregation. In junior high school I was sent to study hall while the class practiced the anthem for graduation. I could stand with the other 200 plus students and mouth the words, but couldn't sing or I would ruin the anthem. (About fifteen others got the same treatment.) But here in my middle age plus years, I was given a starring role BECAUSE of my poor voice. My friend had seen my ability to sing badly and found a way to use it for good. My talents had been recognized and brought to the front. I will never be ashamed of my singing voice again. God gave me this voice. You'll have to listen to it.

SENIOR CITIZEN OW-IES

One of the worst things about having an empty nest is that no one is around to blame things on. For example, if a light is left on, a door not shut, or a phone left off the hook, whom can we blame it on if the kids are all grown and gone? Since always blaming the spouse doesn't help a marriage, some of the fault has to fall back on your own little back.

When the kids do come to visit and bring their offspring, then you can store up a bunch of excuses for the future. Something is missing? One of the children must have looked at it and put it someplace else. There's a spot on the rug? The baby must have spit up or dropped a cookie there. Surely, none of these things could be from our own awkwardness or carelessness.

By the same token, the worst hurts are the ones that we inflict upon ourselves. For four days I nursed a sore thumb because of my own lack of coordination. During a rain storm I rushed to get to the dentist. (That was my first mistake. Who should rush when they are going to a dentist?) As I stepped through the sliding door of our breeze way, my rain bonnet started to blow off. I had pushed the door toward the shut position, but because I was distracted by the rain bonnet problem, I neglected to pull my hand away from the sliding screen door. As a result, I got a nasty blow and cut to my wrist just above the thumb. It was one of those pains that almost make you sick for a moment before easing up some.

Not wanting to be late, I ignored the pain and with tears stinging my eyes went ahead for my appointment. Dr. Bunton did share a band-aid with me and had the courtesy not to laugh at my awkwardness.

I couldn't blame the door. I couldn't blame anyone else since I was all alone. If I got myself injured in such a stupid way, I just had to recognize that my ability to walk and chew gum might be fading a little. It hurt for a long time. I thought that I would at least have a bright bruise to show everyone to gain sympathy, but the only sign was a slight discoloration that isn't much different from all the other brown spots on my skin.

Another time, my publisher invited me to stay with her in a plush condominium. I tried out the sauna in the bathroom and was relaxing in the water when the phone rang. Sliding doors must be a hazard for me. The tub had sliding glass doors around it, and you guessed it, as I was getting out in a hurry to answer the phone, the closing glass door caught my ankle as I pulled it across the top of the tub. It really hurt! I didn't tell anyone about that mishap and again since no bruises appeared, I had to bear my soreness in solitude.

When children get hurt they immediately want a band-aid, and a kiss to ease the pain of the 'ow-ie.' I suppose I am in my second childhood because I also enjoy a little sympathy when I get hurt. When I cause

my own pain, I need extra sympathy. Something like,
"That must have really hurt. Things like that happen
to me all the time, too. I hope it feels better soon."

What I usually get is, "You did WHAT? How did
you get in such a fix?" This is often followed by gales
of laughter, or at least a smile and chuckle.

In my middle age plus, supposedly mature, years,
I should be able to take care of myself, have enough
sense to be safe, and slow down enough that all parts
of my body stay in sync with each other. If I don't,
then I should at least be woman enough to bear my
pain in silence and not seek sympathy. But there is
still a part of each of us that still 'wants Mommy.'

My mother was not one to give a whole lot of sympathy when we got hurt. She usually told us to get up
and try it again, or to be more careful next time. My
older siblings also exhorted me to quit being a cry baby
and hush. I guess I am still feeling somewhat deprived
of my allotted dose of sympathy.

I'm a big girl now and can take care of myself,
usually. But when things go wrong I could still use a
hug. Would you like to see the mark on my thumb?

IT'S THE LITTLE THINGS THAT GET TO YOU

Do you ever have one of those days when everything that happens irritates you? I don't have them very often, but today was the day.

First, I was standing in line at the store when a clerk in another aisle said, "I can take care of you over here, Honey." Now that doesn't sound like anything to get irritated about does it? Unless you are middle age plus and she has just called a man in front of you, "Sir."

The older I get the more I hear people, particularly salespeople, calling me "Honey" or "Darling." It isn't because I have suddenly become so appealing that these sweet words just can't help but pop out. No, it is because they see me as a 'little old lady' that one must be nice to. I doubt that many salespeople would call a fifty-year-old professional woman, "Honey," unless it was a family member or close friend. But a middle age plus professional woman often gets that treatment.

I know they mean to be nice, and so far I haven't snapped back at anyone about it. But I guess it boils down to the fact that I am not ready to be seen as a 'little old lady.'

I call my great-grandchildren "Honey," and "Sweetie" all the time as a form of endearment. But they are little children in my family. I even call other little children by these words, but I certainly wouldn't use them for teenagers or adults. Oh well, I think I will survive.

The next thing that irritated me was a bill I got today saying the payment was overdue. Since I was quite certain it was not overdue, I promptly called the 800 number to use if I had questions about the bill. After ten minutes of getting a busy signal, I finally got through—to a message in Spanish. In a minute or so, I was told that if I wanted to hear the message in English I should punch 1. I did and was told to punch in my customer number. I found the number just before being cut off the line and began punching in the ten digits. After that procedure was over, I was given the choice of three other numbers to punch to get what I needed. I punched 3 and got a woman telling me exactly what was on the bill I had just received. Well, I said I got a woman. Actually, I got a recording that said what the bill had said. (Do you suppose they have a recording ready for every customer number in case one calls in?)

At the end of the recording I was given the option of three more numbers, one of which was to talk to a human being. I chose that one. But instead of a live person I got another recording telling me that they were sorry but due to the rush of calls today, an operator was not available to take my call. But I am very important to them and would I please try my call another time. I did, twice. With the same results each time.

304 For Everything There Is a Season

I was distracted from this scenario by my fax machine making noises like it wanted to give me something. Nothing came out. Upon inspection I discovered that during the weekend someone must have turned it off. Just as I was turning it back on, I got a call from the lady who was sending me the fax telling me to turn on the machine. Though I probably added to her irritations for the day, she was very nice about it.

A week ago I had a potato explode in the oven as I was preparing supper. I didn't take time to clean it up right then because the oven was too hot. Then today forgetting all about the mess within. I turned on the oven to preheat it for some canned biscuits. This oversight added a nice burnt crumb smell to our evening that went well with my mood.

I knew by now it was too late to try my credit card call again. I started to straighten up my papers and get them ready to tackle again another day. In anger I again looked at the offending bill and saw a notation I had overlooked earlier. Maybe it was a good thing I couldn't get through on my calls. I would have ruined another person's day because I just found out that I really did owe what they said I did.

It's bad enough to be dunned for being late in a payment, but it's worse when it is your own fault. I'd still like to try to get through the maze of punching numbers. I want to see if the woman would call me "Honey."

MY MOTHER TOLD ME
THERE'D BE DAYS LIKE THIS

Today I woke up with plans to do a lot of paper work about my responsibilities with the United Methodist Women. Next, I planned to prepare for the speech I will be giving in Jefferson City tomorrow. I know what I am going to say, but I want to get it better organized. It is a subject I know very well—AGING!

After I got things ready for my speech I was going to load the car and write an article for Friday's paper. I had even bought a roast to have for supper since I wouldn't be here tomorrow. That would leave left-overs for Lester to eat on while I am gone. I planned to stick that in the oven while I was doing my writing. In short, it would be a very productive day.

The first thing I did wrong (after even getting out of bed, that is!) was to check my e-mail. Suddenly there was a bunch of decisions to make which necessitated writing more e-mails which only confused the issue. It suddenly was imperative that I make plans for the middle of August when I was doing well to make plans for the one day ahead of me. Other people were making their plans based on my plans. I was ready to say I don't have any plans, I will just stay home all month and sulk. But I didn't. We finally got that straightened out so I now know what I will do the middle week of August. What I don't know is what I'll do about the things I need to do today.

To make matters worse, in the middle of all this e-mailing, my computer suddenly told me that the message was not deliverable since I did not have the proper password. After at least two hours of almost constant use, the mechanism decided I'm not qualified! I am qualified, and after a few calls and using different approaches to my mailbox, I got that problem fixed in time to get another message that changed what I earlier thought was settled.

You get the drift. By now I was in no mood to write a cheery article highlighting the joys of being middle age plus. Really, I thought, if I had the wisdom of this age, I would be outside on this beautiful day watching our creative squirrel rob the bird seed from the feeder. Or I could do some yard work to get ready for club that is meeting here next week. Maybe I could even take a nap.

A trip to the car to load some books for tomorrow's presentation reminded me that the gas stations won't be open when I leave in the morning at six a.m. I ran into town, filled the tank with gas, withdrew some money for my trip, and became even farther behind.

However, seeing the humor in all of this I decided I would just use the day as material. You have no idea how much better I feel after talking it over with all of you. It is really very silly to be upset because I have things interrupting me. I should be glad that others want my advice, need to know my plans, or have asked me to share my vast wisdom about getting old(er).

It's great to have friends to share with and it certainly makes life more pleasurable. I thank you for helping me get my day straightened out.

While I was writing this I got a phone call from my granddaughter. She needs me to take care of her baby tonight for about three hours. I had agreed to do this a couple weeks ago when she was considering enrolling her older daughter in Brownies. Sure, I can keep the baby for a few hours. But suddenly it is today she needs me!

Well, I did get the roast in the oven!

TAKE TWO ASPIRINS AND DRINK LOTS OF FLUIDS

Have you escaped the flu bug? Many have not. I don't know if I am really sick or have a very good imagination. Our two great-granddaughters were sick, and I have been with them quite a bit. After each visit I feel all the symptoms but know I have to go to this meeting, make this phone call, do an interview, or write an article. I soon find out that I'm not really sick after all. That is, I realize it until I think about it again. Then here come the symptoms.

One of my good friends saw me at the grocery store on a day when I needed to wash my hair and hadn't taken time to do much about other grooming chores. She sympathized with me because she thought I looked tired. I had been feeling fine, but then I suddenly realized, "Yes, I am very tired. I better take it easy today." Another time over the phone she thought I sounded like I had a cold. And sure enough, I soon imagined a sore throat. Maybe my imagination helps when I am writing, but it gets a little overactive when I apply it to the condition of my health.

I vividly remember one time in kindergarten I cried at school and said that I didn't feel well. The teacher called my mother who had to walk the mile to Janney School in Washington, D.C. to get me. My mother told the teachers to have me start walking home and she would meet me. (The one family car was downtown where my father worked and, even if it had been home, my mother hated to drive it in the city.) I felt very guilty because I didn't really know if I was sick or not.

The die was cast. I started the long walk home. When I saw my mother at the other end of the long hill on River Road, I sat down on the curb to wait for her. I expected her to be upset with me. She wasn't, of course. I actually was sick and running a fever. But I still remember that guilty feeling I had for saying that I was sick.

Other times when I was sick during the school year, I could have easily been guilty because I felt fine. School policy made me stay out two full weeks with the mumps. Actually, a neighbor girl who also had the mumps came over and played with me because neither one of us felt bad.

I had the measles in the summer when we had threshers at the farm. This was when the owners of the machines stayed in tents on the grounds and were our 'guests' for three meals a day. My mother had to feed them plus the twenty or so neighbors who worked through the day and were there for the noon meal. I can imagine how much time my mother had to cater to the needs of a five-year-old with the measles. My dim memory is that she sent Ellen who was eight years old to see about me. She didn't want to miss out on any of the excitement and didn't stay long. I survived, and so did my mother, but her memories of the old days never included fondness for feeding threshers.

My mother's ideas of treating a sick child included first a bit of anger that we dared to get sick. Then she relied heavily on camphor oil, Vicks, hot water bottles, salt and soda gargle, and serving us soup on a tray in our bedroom. She tried to read a story or two to us when we were small and really sick, but her duties in our large family did not allow much time to pamper the sick one. As I remember it, we stayed in our bedrooms when we were sick and didn't lounge on the living room couch or have pallets fixed on the floor so we could be nearer to her work in the kitchen.

I do remember one time when she bundled me up in heavy clothes, wrapped me in a blanket, and set me outside at the bottom of the back porch steps to sit in the sun, thinking that would be good for me. It was so rare for me to be home at that time of day with no other siblings around that I can still remember the silence of the neighborhood and the comforting feel of the sun on my face. I don't know what my illness was, but I was glad she chose that treatment for me.

I don't take after my mother in this respect. I pampered my kids when they were sick and don't ignore my own illnesses as she did. I hope my life can be as healthy as hers was. But first I must decide if I have the flu or not!

PICKET FENCES OR TRAILER HITCHES

On a trip through the Ozarks, I noticed several restored log cabins which were being used to promote a business or to set the scene for a nostalgic visit to the past. These scenes usually had the log cabin with flowers around the door, a couple of rocking chairs on the porch, cheery curtains hanging in the widows, and maybe even a picket fence enclosing the scene.

Those who actually lived in log cabins in the past probably remember a different scene. Instead of flowers in the lawn, there were probably chickens or other fowl making the area around the house part of their grazing land. The chairs on the porch were straight chairs with cane bottoms that the men tilted back to sit in while waiting for a meal to be served. There was not much idle time for the hard-working Ozark folk who lived in these cabins.

My husband was born in a log cabin and lived in one until he was twelve. Then his family built a four-room home. He and his siblings don't agree exactly on the lay out of the cabin, but Lester and his eldest brother both remembered an open space with a floor and roof that separated the kitchen from the living room/bedroom combination. The other two siblings insist that there was not an open area. They all agree, however, that it is not the floor plan they would choose for their present homes.

Admiration and fond memories are reserved for the people of that era and not for the hard life style of the times.

Today, those who need to find low cost housing often decide upon living in a house trailer. These can be fixed up nicely with a lawn and flowers around them to provide pleasant living.

I wonder if, like the log cabin, future commercial sites wanting to set the stage for a nostalgic visit to the turn of this century will use an old house trailer in their setting. It is serving the same function as the rugged log cabin did at the beginning of the twentieth century for hard-working folk who needed an inexpensive place for their family to live. However, it is hard for us to think that anyone would ever chose to use these manufactured houses in a display to create nostalgia.

When women were searching through barns and flea markets to find big black pots to put in their lawn for flowers, my mother was amazed. She said she couldn't wait to get such pots out of her yard when she no longer had to heat water in them to do the weekly clothes washing. Likewise, she had no reluctance to let the three-doored icebox make room for an automatic refrigerator.

Many restaurants and business places today decorate with old tools, old kitchen utensils, old styles of shoes, hats, or furniture. This sets the stage for hours of conversation about Mama's kitchen, Papa's workshop, or even our childhood homes. Our yearning to recreate these memories never goes so far that we actually change our lifestyle back to match that of those times. The memory was a nice place to visit, but we wouldn't want to live there.

What will be the fond memories of life today? Will we revere the computer as a sign of an era that has become outmoded in future generations? Will the drive-through quick food restaurants be an icon to represent this age? Or will our children and grand-children bore their families with tales of how hard it was to drive for hours in cars whose tires had to re-main on the highways as they traveled?

Things from the past take on an aura of rever-ence for the inheritance we gain from those times. Sometimes we almost forget that they are just things. We get them mixed in our minds with the beloved people who lived in those times and places. We never want to forget those who have gone before us. The things of their times help us remember.

Maybe that is why when we were shopping for a modular home several years ago we were drawn to-ward the ones with the fake log exterior.

TABLE FOR ONE

Lester and I were sitting in a restaurant when a woman walked in alone. The hostess asked her, "Only one?" The woman nodded yes and was seated. I began thinking about the question the hostess asked. It implied that maybe one was not a proper number or that surely there must be someone else with this woman.

In this age of professional women traveling worldwide by themselves, why should there be any stigma to a woman eating alone? Yet I have heard others say that they do as I do when I don't have a dining partner. I go by the drive-through windows, order some food, and take it to a park to eat in my car. I have enjoyed many pleasant meals at the top of the hill in Spring Street Park with my radio tuned to classical music, looking at the view down the hill, and pulling all the onions out of my hamburger because I forgot to tell the server to omit them.

When I am traveling alone, I usually park at a restaurant as far away from the building as possible to get some exercise walking. After using the facilities, I order my food to go and return to the car to continue driving as I eat. It helps pass the next half hour on the road. The little walk gives me a break.

But part of the reason is I hate to eat alone, especially in public.

Except when I was sick in bed and had my meal brought up to me on a tray, I don't think I ever ate a meal alone until I went to college. In our big family there was always a crowd at meal time. Even when the older siblings left home there were three or four at each meal. In college I lived in a boarding house the first two years with many people eating together. Then I moved to a rooming house where I had to go elsewhere to eat. Or I cooked for myself in a basement make-shift kitchen. Sometimes, tiring of my peanut butter and jelly sandwiches, I walked to the bus station to get a cheap meal of tuna salad sandwiches and hot chocolate.

Although maturity has made me more aware of good nutrition, I still rarely go into a restaurant, sit down, and eat a full meal when I am alone.

I don't know why this is. I am not afraid. I am not embarrassed at my lack of an escort. I just prefer to be private when I am alone.

I am reminded of the wonderful people in our community who are, or were, the last of their families. The recent death of Dorothy Hill who left no heirs causes me to try to imagine what it would be like to have no family members left. I don't think I will ever have this situation. I can boast having a family numbering close to a hundred, counting the children, grandchildren, great-grandchildren, and great-great-grandchildren of my parents. The family Lester and I have created now numbers over twenty. My family by marriage is also fairly large.

But I also am aware that our community has gained by some of our former citizens having no family heirs. The Moss Trust, the donations that Dorothy Hill made to her favorite programs, and the years of volunteer hours put in by capable persons such as Helen Margaret Warren, who created her own family out of the staff and other volunteers in her chosen agencies, are all examples of ways we all have become heirs of those who had no blood family remaining.

I need to get over my dislike of solitary dining because I know there is enjoyment in people-watching as I eat. Even if Lester and I are together we often are not in constant conversation but are each lost in our own thoughts and enjoying watching the other families and individuals who are in the restaurant. I should get the same relaxation when I need to eat and have no companion. I am going to make an effort to do just that. Since hamburgers are not the best diet to eat day after day, I will sit down to order a meal with vegetables, salad, and, of course, dessert.

Because I know the time will come when I will need to answer yes when St. Peter asks, "Only one?"

Estrella & Alejandro Rivera
July 7, 2007
Wedding Images Available for Ordering
Online After July 20, 2007
www.lozoya.com/online_ordering
Log-in Password: Estrella
Questions? Call Lozoya Studios at:
(505) 243-1007
www.lozoya.com

MID-WINTER
EVENING CRISIS

It is happening again just as it does every year about this time. It couldn't have come at a worse time, either. It has come when the weather has made me a likely target, and my resistance is weakened. Last year when this happened, I made plans to keep it from happening again. I'm not sure they will work. I didn't realize what this month-long period of cold and snow would do to me. Last year's episode came even though the months had not been nearly as wintry. This year with this weather I'm not sure what will be the result.

You see, what has happened is, the seed catalogs have arrived. Two of them came together this very day from different green houses. I am sitting in my house with a robe over my feet, looking out at a cold, cloudy landscape. Two catalogs in my lap show luscious vegetables, colorful flowers, and a hedge that doesn't need any care to provide an attractive backdrop for the spring flowers the bulb varieties will produce.

Ordering is even easy using the handy form inside or calling the 800 number and giving credit card would visit one of our local greenhouses to purchase a few plants that were already growing well. I'd plant them in pots around the house where all I had to do was water them from time to time.

That was my plan last spring when the seeds, bulbs, and stringy little seedlings arrived not looking at all like the pretty pictures in the catalog.

Although we didn't miss having home grown tomatoes last year, since our generous neighbors shared with us, it would be good to have several tomato plants this year to pick a ripe tomato anytime we wanted one. Also, we are both fond of corn on the cob. One or two rows of sweet corn would be plenty for us to have all we need to satisfy our cravings.

The catalogs have several varieties and the words underneath make it sound like these types are much superior to any others. The green beans and okra don't tempt me at all, and I can pass right over the pages that show black-eyed peas. Since one or two sacks of onions is all we would use in an entire year, there is no reason to even think about the pictures on those pages.

So I go deeper into the book to find the things that really tempt me—the flowering bushes that bloom year after year with very little effort. As I look out the window at the snow-covered forsythia bush, I realize that I already have several very nice bushes if they all live through this bitter cold winter.

Will I be able to resist the tempting displays on the shiny pages?

I think I have decided what I will do. I will go buy an amaryllis bulb that will grow in our living room and give me several luscious blooms to cheer up these dark days. I will take good care of my Christmas poinsettia and hope that the red blooms will looked as delightful as those in the pictures. I might even buy one of the early daffodils that show up in the grocery stores a month or more before their cousins appear outside. These purchases may keep me from going wild with the temptations of these flowery displays.

That settles all of my problems but the desire for a few tomatoes and ears of corn. I can buy the seeds right here in town when it is time to plant. That is the best part of it all. Everything that looks so beautiful in the catalogs can be found right here from our neighbor merchants. And their smiles beat any 800 number or dot.com opportunity.

NOW I UNDERSTAND

I have been thinking a lot about my mother-in-law the last two nights. I have been 'puny' with bronchitis. I wake up many times during the night because of my cough, and that is the time I think about my mother-in-law.

When we asked her for gift suggestions, her first reply always was that she would like to have a clock with numbers big enough to read at a distance, one that she could see well enough at night to tell the time. This was before digital clocks with colored, lighted numerals. The best we could find was one with an interior light that somewhat lighted the blocks that fell down in turn to give the time. The numbers on the blocks were not very large and she still couldn't see them well, especially at night.

We were busy parents with jobs, family obligations, and church duties. We didn't see why it mattered whether she could see the time when she awoke at night. After all, she didn't have any place to go the next day. She could stay in bed late and nothing would matter. So why worry about the time in the middle of the night?

During this episode, I am having with bronchitis, I keep a glass of water by my bed to take a drink to curb the coughing a bit. Three nights ago I spilled the water all over my vanity, and it saturated the digital clock with the lighted red numerals on it. I wouldn't recommend this treatment for clock-radios because it messed things up quite a bit. We had to unplug the appliance, leaving me with no clock on my side of the bed. There was one on Lester's side, but I couldn't see it unless I sat up in bed. I am used to being able to barely open my eyes and know what time it is by looking at my own clock.

Since I was half sick, I wasn't going anywhere the next day. It didn't matter if I slept late, so why all the concern over the time? That was when I remembered my mother-in-law and realized that her need to know the time was the same as mine. We just want to know.

Now I understand and share many of the concerns and requests of my older relatives. In the past I was either amused or irritated by many of these. Now they seem perfectly normal and necessary.

For example, my father got very annoyed at the small print on the directions on some tools. He was upset enough that sometimes he wouldn't even use the newer tools but continued to use the old stand-bys that he knew how to operate without reading any instructions. We were surprised that this intelligent man felt this way. But a new VCR my family has today has letters and numbers in black, on black, so small that I can't read them without shining a flashlight directly on them. I don't use it very much because it is pretty complicated even if you could read the letters and numbers.

My sister, Miriam, got disturbed when the so-called background music in a public place was so loud that she couldn't hear conversations. When she turned up her hearing aid, it just made the background music more annoying. She still couldn't hear what we were saying. Since it didn't sound loud to us at the time, we thought she could have tried harder to hear if she really wanted to. Recently we took our family out to eat in a local restaurant. Two different times we had to ask the waitress to turn down the volume on the mood-setting music. The only mood it set in me was irritation. I wanted to hear what my family was saying, and no matter how hard I tried, I couldn't hear their conversation.

People that mumble or don't talk loud enough to hear, television shows that switch actions and scenes so often I can't follow the plot, menus that don't offer ordinary food without all the high seasoning so popular these days—these are few of my unfavorite things. They are all complaints that some of my older loved ones also found unpleasant. When it is too late to be patient with their peeves, I now see why.

Tonight when I wake up and can again read the time on the repaired clock-radio, I will ask forgiveness from all who reached middle age plus earlier than I did.

Section Ten

A TIME TO DIE

In spite of days too full of strife
I know that life is good.
And thus since Death is part of life,
I know that Death is good.

IS THERE LIFE
AFTER MEMORIES?

I believe that part of a person's immortality lies in the memories left behind. While remembering something about a friend or a loved one, we continue the influence of that life upon us.

For example, how many times have you heard people who are quite old themselves quote something their mother or father told them? Even though the speaker is well past the age of the parent who gave this advice, the importance of the message is evident. A recent commercial sings, "My mamma told me, you'd better shop around," carries out that idea.

The memory that brings a person to mind usually isn't earth-shaking or a momentous occasion. More often it is triggered by an everyday occurrence.

When I see a particularly beautiful sunset, I remember my Aunt Lyle. She was an avid photographer who took endless pictures of spots of beauty, which she then showed us on slides in endless sessions on her annual visits to the farm. While she was with us, any time there was a pretty sunset, one of us would call to her, "Aunt Lyle, there's a pretty sunset." She would grab her camera to take yet another view of the sun going down behind our Osage orange hedge row.

It was a matter of amusement for us at the time, but now I look at pretty sunsets with fondness for this woman. She left the comforts of her single life in a modern home in Norman, Oklahoma, where she was head of the Home Economics Department of the University of Oklahoma, to come spend a couple of weeks in our farmhouse. Our lack of plumbing and the over-crowded conditions of our large family didn't prevent her from keeping up family ties.

Each month when I first spot the new moon, I remember my sister, Miriam. In the years we spent living as neighbors, we strived to be the first to sight the new moon each month. Then we called the other to announce our discovery. I still 'tell' her each time I see that little sliver of light in the evening sky.

When I bustle around picking up things and putting everything back in place after the children, grand-children, and great-grandchildren leave, I remember my father. He couldn't stand to have anything out of place. Often some item we left behind by accident almost beat us home because he would package it up and mail it to us immediately. It wasn't that he thought we needed it so soon. He just didn't want it left around. Now that I am middle age plus, I understand. I don't mail things, but I do put them away until the next visit.

Sweeping off the front sidewalks always reminds me of my mother. She never wanted grass clippings, leaves, or trash to clutter up the approach to the house. Both in Washington, D.C., and at the farm, she would sweep the front walk and porch at the least sign of debris. I share this impulse, and when I do, I have memories of a great woman.

Seeing a roller coaster ride reminds me of my brother, Vernon, who used to take me with him and our brother, Ralph, on scary rides at Glen Echo Park near Washington. I don't ride them anymore, but I know if he were still alive, he would.

I even evoke memories of special cats or dogs in certain circumstances and enjoy again the animal-human relationship of years gone by.

The big problem with this thinking is, do I lose part of my immortality when there is no one left to remember me? For several generation, stories will be passed down that keep memories alive, but that will eventually stop.

If I try to create some really outstanding memories that will survive after I am gone, I may not succeed because I can never know just what someone else will remember about our relationship. Perhaps the best plan is to just live our everyday lives and hope that somewhere in all the mundane things we do, we are creating memories.

I hope that no one has stored away a memory of how I look when I first wake up each morning. I would rather be forgotten than have that memory preserved.

GLENN THORNTON
1911-1998

The older I get the more I realize how important families are. The death of my brother-in-law, Lester's oldest brother, made a bittersweet gathering of the extended Thornton family that had not occurred for many years. Although the occasion was one of sorrow, there was joy in siblings being together again, of cousins meeting each other for the first time as adult to adult, and of stories flowing easily about the man we had lost and the parents and grandparents of the family.

Since Glenn was thirteen years older than Lester, he was a man in the eyes of his little brother. He helped shape ideas of what manhood was all about, and even taught this younger boy skills of his trade of plumbing, welding, and other mechanical arts. Since all of the siblings attended the School of the Ozarks near Branson, Missouri, when it was a high school, they shared this school's spirit and heritage plus the work ethic the institution instilled in every student. Work was the way to prove your value to others. Glenn worked many a cold night helping someone overcome a plumbing or heating problem.

One of my favorite memories of Glenn was when his second child was a toddler. He was installing a refrigerator for his mother at her farm in southeastern Taney County. This was well before the area was a tourist mecca. This farm was a long drive over gravel roads from Branson where Glenn lived. He had brought this first refrigerator his mother ever had to her home on a Sunday afternoon when many family members were present.

Glenn lay on his back making adjustments to the refrigerator, while people were snacking on food spread out on the table in the adjoining room. Glenda went to the table and got a handful of slaw, took it to her father, and popped it in his mouth. Glenn thanked her for the gesture. The little girl was so pleased that she kept repeating the act to the amusement of the family. Finally Glenn looked up at me and whispered, "Can you stop that process from the other end. I don't have the heart to tell her I can't stand anymore slaw!"

While the family was together for the funeral, we agreed that it was a shame that we hadn't gathered more often. When Lester's mother was alive everyone jammed into her little home in Branson where she moved after she was widowed. Every Christmas, Thanksgiving, and often on her birthday, all the kids and grandkids came together for a big meal in the home where there was very little room to move about. Thankfully there was a large porch around the upstairs of the house and the group spilled out onto this area to visit and even to eat when the weather allowed it. But when the mother had to move to a nursing home, these get-togethers stopped as we each made our visits separately to spread out her enjoyment longer.

As we joined together as family to say farewell to the first of the siblings to die, we realized the comfort and joy in just being together. We made many promises as we began leaving for our various homes. We will plan a family reunion to be together when it isn't a special or sad day. We will drop by to visit one another more often. We exchanged e-mail addresses with promises of keeping in touch.

During the drive home I reflected on the day and its meaning to me, an in-law. I realized that although blood is certainly thicker than water, a family that has been part of my life for over half a century is an important part of who I am.

Glenn was true to form. Just as he brought refrigeration to his mother and spent the family gathering working to be sure that his mother's need was met, his death brought warmth and love to a family who had neglected to stay in touch as often as they should.

And we didn't serve any cole slaw.

CROSSES ON THE HIGHWAY OF LIFE

I have noticed several places on the highways where someone has placed a small white cross with artificial flowers around it. Sometime there is a little fence with many decorations inside the area. Other times the cross stands alone with perhaps one or two flowers on or beside it. I noticed one arrangement fastened to the side of a bridge railing.

I know these crosses mark where someone was killed on the highway. They are intended to have a double purpose. One is to keep a special sacred spot where a loved one has died. The other is to remind those who are passing by that accidents happen, and we should all drive carefully.

I have heard that there is some question about the safety of these signs. Some say that looking at the crosses distracts motorists. It is better to keep your eyes on the road and not to look at details on the roadside, but I doubt that many have been distracted enough to be in danger.

On a recent trip I began thinking about where different loved ones of mine had taken their last breath. If I were to erect a small cross at every such spot, I would have to put some in rooms of family homes, quite a few in nursing homes and in hospitals. Imagine the downer for patients or residents of institutions if little crosses adorned every bed where someone had died. Intellectually, we know that people have died there, but we don't want to be reminded of it each time we are admitted to the hospital.

There are other deaths in our lives besides our physical ones. I have many ideas that die before I get around to following up on them. This is especially true of ideas I have in the middle of the night. Brilliant thoughts come to me when I am in bed. I think that my idea has probably enough merit to make us rich for the rest of our lives. Then in the morning, I either cannot even remember what the idea was, or in the light of day it doesn't sound so wonderful after all.

Perhaps I need to put some little crosses by my bed to remind me to go slow when speeding through a thought. Ideas have died here.

Relationships can die even before the participants have actually left this earth. Divorce courts and counseling offices probably could erect many little crosses to commemorate the death of a once promising relationship.

Possibly my biggest need to put up markers is for the demise of good intentions. I am certain that I will carry out a good deed immediately, but things intervene, and the action never happens. I am going to write letters, send cards, visit my neighbors, invite friends in for a meal, write thank you notes promptly, drink less Dr. Pepper, eat more broccoli, or get my desk organized. But I never get to them.

Where would I put the crosses to remind me of

the loss of these good intentions? Maybe I could hang a tiny one inside my glasses' frame so that no matter where I looked or what I saw, I would realize that one more impulse died.

Or, perhaps as I pass the markers on the roadside, what I should do is incorporate all these other things that have died into a thought. When I see one or two little crosses, I could share a kind thought for that person's loved ones, but also remind myself of all the losses my laziness and procrastination have caused me. Each tragic accident could jolt me to re-examine myself more often and realize what I may have lost.

However, such thoughts only add to the distraction of seeing the crosses. If I am already driving I don't want to be burdened with self-doubts about my life. I think it would be healthier to forget about these other deaths in my life and go on just as I have been.

Maybe it's better to simply look ahead and mind my own business. I certainly don't want other people to know all the things I should have done or how many good things have died because of something I didn't do.

IN MY MERRY OLDSMOBILE

I am in mourning. No loved one has died nor has a beloved pet left us. But a car that has been in our family for sixteen years is being crushed today. Cars and memories are so closely linked in this motorized age that this white Oldsmobile Omega has seemed like one of the family. It was not actually Lester's and my car until just the past few weeks, but it was the car of my late sister, Miriam. Since we had lived as neighbors for so long, the car also became an important part of our lives.

My first clear memory of the car was when my sister, Ellen, and I drove it to a family reunion in Cleveland where Miriam met us as she was returning from one of her many trips. Following the reunion, the three of us drove the car back to Missouri. Ellen and I tried to keep Miriam's mind off of the long drive by playing games and carrying on animated conversation. We each wanted to return home that night, but Miriam, the seasoned traveler, wanted to be more leisurely by stretching out the trip a bit longer. We reached St. Louis before she realized how far we had gone during the day and agreed that the few more miles to Lebanon where Ellen lived would be the wise thing to do.

After Lester and I retired and lived next door, Miriam and I often shared rides to meetings especially at night, sometimes with me driving her car . We used her car when one of ours was in the shop, or when company visiting need more wheels than we could offer. I was as comfortable at the wheel of her Omega as I was at one of our own vehicles.

During the last few years of Miriam's life, I drove for her all the time, usually in her car, as we went for groceries, to the doctor, or to club meetings. In her last month, I had a harrowing experience in the car. I was taking her to the doctor for a regular visit when soon after I got the car started, she lost consciousness. I didn't know whether to stop and call for the ambulance or speed ahead to the doctor's office. Since we were already headed that way, I drove as quickly as I could while holding her erect in the passenger seat with one arm and driving with the other. I ran into the clinic and yelled for the nurse who thankfully was free and came to my rescue. After Miriam spent a day or two in the hospital, I was able to take her back home in the same car. That was the last time she ever rode in it.

After her death, our daughter bought the car from the estate and took it to her home in Texas. This seemed to be a happy solution since Susan enjoyed having her aunt's car, and we knew it was still in the family and would come home for visits, just as children do when they leave home. However, it evidently didn't care for Texas weather. It soon began to cause all sorts of expensive problems. Susan brought the car home. We tried to remedy some of its ills until it became too expensive to be sensible. Yesterday, we sold it to the junk yard where the workmen said it would be crushed today.

As we were taking the personal things from the trunk and glove compartment, I visualized all the pleasant times spent in the car. Tears came to my eyes when I picked some bits of paper from the passenger front seat where I remembered Miriam sitting during the last ride in her little Omega.

Now you can see me bussing around in our new car enjoying all the bells and whistles. Since we traditionally keep a car for many years, I realize this may be the vehicle in which someone takes me for my own last ride.

BITTERSWEET THANKSGIVING

On Thanksgiving Day, 2000, when we were all thinking of things we were thankful for, we gave somewhat sad thanks for being a small part of the life of my sister-in-law, Dorothy, whose memorial service was held that day. I was not able to join her three daughters and their families for this service but had my own time of remembering this vivacious young woman whom I met in the early 1940s.

My brother, Vernon, had married while he was in Rochester, New York, and brought his bride home to meet the family. My mother let me skip school for this occasion so that I could drive her to the Union Station in Washington, D.C. to meet the couple.

Dorothy was an only child with only one cousin. She had been raised around Rochester and loved the Great Lakes and the northern part of our country. Now she was meeting her husband's large, Midwestern-rooted family for the first time. Since she was not much older than I was, we got along fine. When she and Vernon went to Mt. Vernon to sight-see that afternoon, Dorothy invited me to go with them. That gesture was all it took to sell me on this new family member.

Later they moved to a suburb of Cleveland, Ohio,

where Vernon was an engineer with NASA and Dorothy was busy raising Jane, Ann, and Beth. It was a treat to visit in their home because there was always something fun going on. Dorothy's sense of humor and liveliness enriched our times together.

She was a good sport about coming to our family reunions and visits in Missouri even though she did not care for farm life and our flat countryside. Once when she looked out at the beautiful (to us) field of corn across the driveway from the house, she remarked that she would hate to have to look at that day after day. However, she did learn to appreciate our home roots and even after Vernon died at an early age, she continued to join us at all family gatherings until her health made this impossible.

This bundle of pep and energy was gradually being imprisoned by Huntington's disease. As the years wore on, her active, alert mind could not communicate with her family and friends. The disease robbed her of her muscular ability to even form words, while at the same time made her body perform erratic movements beyond her control.

Her daughter, son-in-law, and two grandsons became her care givers for weekly trips away from the nursing home where she spent her last years. Her good spirit remained and showed through the limitations of her disease. Her other two daughters and families were also frequent visitors.

In any death there is always an element of guilt in those left behind. I regret not sending more letters and cards or going to visit.

Now on the day of her memorial service, I give thanks for the extra zest that she brought into our family. While definitely declaring that she was not a

Gray but a Champlin, she adjusted to this big farm family and gave us the gift of three nieces, three grand-nephews, and two wonderful nephews-in-law to continue giving our family that extra flavor they acquired from Dorothy.

For that I give thanks.

DECORATION DAY

Since my peonies are in bloom, it must be getting close to Memorial Day. These large blossoms are a favorite flower to take to the cemetery on what used to be called Decoration Day.

My parents did not decorate graves as a rule. They believed that gifts to charities or special acts of kindness to living persons were more suitable ways to honor the memory of a loved one. Yet my mother tried to see that the grave of her old friend and neighbor, Mrs. Horn, had flowers on it. Mrs. Horn, who became like a grandmother to all of the Gray children would see that the proper flowers were put on the graves of all her former neighbors including my grandparents' graves. Since our family was still in Washington, D.C. on Memorial Day, Mrs. Horn felt she was helping us out by this act. After her death and my parents' retirement back to our farm, my mother repaid this courtesy by decorating her grave.

My husband's mother, however, worked for days to prepare flowers and other decorations to put on her family graves in Taney County, Missouri. The day was commemorated by family gatherings, church services, and 'dinner on the ground' at the cemeteries. Everyone walked through the cemetery grounds looking at the flowers and reminiscing about those they were honoring. It was a community affair as well as a family gathering. As long as her health allowed, my mother-in-law went to each cemetery where members of her family were buried.

Lester's grandmother, who died when his mother was only fourteen, was buried in a cemetery that we could no longer reach by road. Isolated in a pasture on private property of a neighbor, it was somewhat neglected. Many years our family tried to clear some of the underbrush away from the graves. The chore was not pleasant as the area was heavily infested with ticks and poison ivy. After one episode when our toddler daughter's white socks suddenly became polka dotted with yearling ticks, I stayed with the children in the car parked in the neighbor's barnyard instead of making the trek up the hill.

When we are middle age plus, we realize that eventually some provision for our own burial must be made, but many of us put it off until it becomes someone else's decision. I don't want to have a tombstone with my name on it placed before my death, but I can see that it might be a service to the family.

If I did fix my tombstone ahead of time, I wonder if I would get any flowers on Memorial Day?

A FINAL TRIBUTE TO MY BROTHER RALPH

In 1964 on April 3, my brother, Ralph, wrote a poem in honor of our father whom we buried that day. Thirty-six years later on that day, I received a phone call from my niece telling me that Ralph himself might not live out the day. A cancer that was not supposed to have grown claimed his life in his eighty-fifth year.

Ralph was the poet, the artist, the sensitive one in the family. I remember as a small child seeing him, a teenager, sitting at the edge of the lawn, petting a chicken and feeding it bits of pancakes from breakfast. Mama wanted him to wring its neck so she could cook it for dinner, but Ralph, the tenderhearted one, couldn't bring himself to do it. I think Mama finally did it herself.

I knew I could always have a shoulder to cry on if I went to Ralph with my problems because he understood my heartbreaks. In fact, I took over the role of crybaby when he outgrew it, though he never outgrew the tenderness the name implied.

I have always been very proud of this brother (as I am of all my siblings) because he was the editor of

the *National Geographic School Bulletin* for years and
then later of the *Geographic World* magazine. In the
summers, he and Jean, and their four children traveled the United States while Ralph gathered material for articles in upcoming National Geographic
books and magazines. Our family was even privileged
to be included in one article about canoeing in the
Ozarks. Our children thought that having this famous
uncle was really exciting.

After retiring from the National Geographic organization, Ralph and Jean moved to a retirement
community in Brevard, North Carolina, where he got
involved with literary groups and renewed his writing of poetry.

This big brother of whom I am so proud was more
pleased that he published his book of poems the same
year that my book was published than he was of the
earlier stories for the magazine. Since our sister, Ellen,
also had a book that came out about the same time,
Ralph took great pride in the fact that all three of us
published a book in 1999. I am grateful that this happened and that we shared the heady experience together.

The knowledge that Ralph was proud of my ac-
complishments after all the years of my looking up to
him was one of the best things about having my own
book. When Ellen and I visited him in Brevard, he
showed us off to all of his friends as if we were something special. This is a wonderful memory for me.

When each of us finally learned the ins and outs
of e-mail correspondence, we kept the messages flying back and forth. Eventually, they got longer and
more philosophical as we journeyed down memory lane
together via e-mail. I probably came to know Ralph

better his last year than I did all the previous ones when we were living in the same house or visiting back home at the same time. I am thankful that I didn't erase a single one of our 'conversations' and I printed them out to keep as precious heirlooms of two siblings, separated by distance and age, but together in love of words and family.

As his children and grandchildren gathered around his bed before he died, I had the privilege of speaking to him on the phone and hearing him say my name when Judy told him who had called. I told him how much Lester and I each loved him and how proud we were of him. He heard me. He knew we were thinking and praying for him, and it helped each of us.

There is no sadness like losing a loved one, but we take heart in the years of shared experiences, joys, and tears, and feel blessed that this brother, who wrote a poem for our father on that April day years ago, can be known by all of us as we read his poetic autobiography, *Behold This Dreamer*. Thanks for a lifetime of pride and love, Ralph. We cherish our memories of you.

MEMORIES OF
A SPECIAL LADY

Being the youngest in a large family can be an unhappy position because I am living through the losses of beloved family members who are older than I am.

We received word that our sister-in-law, Jean Gray, the widow of our brother Ralph, passed away in her room in the nursing home in Brevard, North Carolina, where she lived for several years. She had been very lonely since Ralph died because he had visited her regularly twice each day from his apartment in the retirement village where they moved several years ago. Their children were not close geographically, but each of the four tried to visit often. But it was not the same.

I first met Jean when Ralph brought her home for a family meal after they met in a poetry club at the University of Maryland. Although I had very attractive sisters, I thought I had never met anyone as pretty as Jean. I was in junior high school at the time and appreciated the attention she gave to a gawky kid.

After their marriage and the birth of their first child, they lived in a basement apartment across a large lawn from our family. I delighted in going over each afternoon after school to talk over the day's events with Jean and to 'help' take care of the baby. Jean had been an English teacher during the year after she finished college and Ralph was still in school. She helped me with English assignments and was encouraging as I first tried my hand at creative writing.

Since she was born in Canada and her parents came from Scotland, Jean gave me an understanding of different ways and different places.

Throughout all the years that Ralph wrote for the *National Geographic*, she was a willing traveler with her husband, taking the children along on cross-country trips for a story he was writing. They camped often, or later drove one of the first motor homes available. They had to have several clean outfits ready at any time for picture taking since they couldn't have picture after picture of the children wearing the same clothes. Naturally this chore fell to Jean, who had to depend on coin laundries to keep the family looking fresh and clean.

I never heard Jean complain or criticize anyone. She was always the peacemaker as well as the chief cheerleader for her husband and for the four children. Grandchildren and great grandchildren gave her joy and pride in the later years of her life.

A poem Ralph wrote about his wife, published in his book of poetry, summarizes much of her life.

MY ONCE AND FUTURE QUEEN

The boys in college called her Queen;
  Said she'd be hard to win.
She drew a line that ruled them out,
  And left me snugly in.
As prince-consort in her domain
  I traveled on to lofty things,
Accepting ever her queenly gift
  Of wind beneath my wings.
Her realm reached out to distant coasts
  And inward to her family's care;
But time walked through a hidden door
  And stripped her kingdom bare.

Now one sparse room defines her world
  Yet still to her a noble manse;
  Every item ordained its place;
Water daily for her potted plants.

It pleases me that the Queen and her Prince are together this Christmas as they have been every Christmas for the past sixty-four years. I hope there will be some poetry read.

GOOD-BYE MAMA

I wrote the following in 1969 shortly after the death of my mother, Iola Pearl Welch Gray, to send in a Round Robin to my siblings. I close with this tribute.

She was a woman for all seasons.

"Good-bye Mama," and an answering hoarse whisper, "Bye." This was the last word I heard Mama speak. I returned later and spoke to her and was with her and two of my sisters when she died, but this was the last word she spoke to me. Actually it was probably more to Lester than to me because she always appreciated my husband's visits and tried hard to be clear and gracious when he was her visitor.

It seems appropriate to me that this last word I heard my mother speak should be a farewell. Not because she was dying, but because this was the way she lived. Like all good mothers she raised her eight children to get along without her. No tied apron strings in our house! We were all encouraged to have experiences and adventures independently even though we were a close family and shared many hours together.

Thinking back over the times Mama and I had said good-bye to each other, I remember most clearly the times it was hard for one or the other of us to say good-bye. Like the first time that I felt really alone.

For some reason, in the midst of this big family, I was the only one available to walk the quarter mile to the mailbox one hot summer day when I was five. I had walked this road many times with an older brother or sister, or with Mama, but never alone. I don't re-member the circumstances, but I remember Mama standing at the front door as I walked down the ce-ment walk to the long driveway up to the mailbox. I must have been afraid to leave because I remember her saying, "I'll watch you as you go. Be sure and get all the letters. You can do it." With that moral sup-port I started up the hot driveway. I looked back often to see if Mama was really watching, and she was! I recall the feel of the hot dust under my bare feet and the fear that some varmint might be lurking under the driveway bridge (really only a culvert, but a bridge to me). It didn't occur to me to give up and come back. My mother said I could do it, so I could.

Unfortunately, the mail hadn't passed when I reached the box, and I knew I was in for a long wait. I picked a seat under the shade of an Osage orange tree in the fence row and wiggled my feet in the dust in the bottom of the ditch. The road stretched out miles to the south, and I watched anxiously to see the tell-tale cloud of dust that would show a car was approach-ing. I have no idea how long the wait really was, but it is etched in my memory as an eternity. Eventually, however, the mail did come. I received the *Kansas City Times* and yesterday evening's *Star* and a letter from Papa who was still in Washington at work while we were on the farm.

I started up the drive toward the house with the mailman's words of praise ringing in my ears, "Well, I see the Grays have another helper now." The walk home didn't seem long, and the prize I carried made me feel like a conquering hero. Sure enough, as I crawled under the 'bob wire' fence and cut across the lawn for the last stretch of the walk, I could see Mama watching as she said she would. I had gone out alone with her assurance that I could do it and returned to find her calm acceptance of the fact that I did okay. Of course I would do fine. I was one of her children, wasn't I?

Later, in Washington, when Ellen started junior high and had a different route to walk to school than I did in the third grade, again I can remember starting forth in some anxiety, so unused to being alone. As usual Mama stood in the door and watched me. I crossed Western Avenue and climbed the bank to cross the empty lot to another street that started the mile walk to school. I knew the way well as I had walked it with Ellen every day for the past two years, but this was different. I started to cross back to the house, but Mama called across the street, "Go on now. You'll be late," and then, "Bye," and I went. (I must admit that sometimes I could work this being late bit and get Mama to get the Buick out and drive me to school. But her terror of city traffic, and her country-style driving made her adhere closely to the firm, "Go on now.")

When Kathryn, the first to marry, left home, Ellen and I would spend our Easter vacations with her in the suburbs of New York City. The year finally came when Ellen was not going and I was to take the trip alone. I clearly remember Mama and me beginning the long bus and streetcar ride across Washington to the Union Station about two hours too early. Mama had a fear of being late anywhere. My small brown suitcase was a badge of my importance as we changed from bus to streetcar and finally arrived at the Union Station. I was glad to have Mama handle the mechanics of buying the ticket and finding me my seat, but was furious with her when she told the porter where I was going and to watch out for me! But the thrill of waving good-bye out the window of a moving train was almost unbearable as I watched Mama grow smaller in the dim enclosure over the tracks. My thrill quickly dissolved when I found that my seat mate was a vacationing junior high school teacher!

There were other times when Mama left us at home as she left on a trip. She left with a calm good-bye, assured that her family would take care of itself in her absence. I felt the seriousness when she left us to go say good-bye to her own mother (and arrived too late to be able to do so). I felt that I should be feeling more grief because my grandmother was dying. But the calmness in Mama as she said good-bye dispelled my guilt feelings. She assured us we would be fine in her absence. And we were. We could manage nicely without her, although we were always happy to see her return.

Papa was gone so much on his job during my child-hood that I would lose count of whether he was home or away. However, I remember his homecomings more than his departures. He often brought us a jar of stick candy that was sold in railroad stations at the time. They were of a variety of colors and had lovely hollow tubes inside them that would bring the juice from the